'If you've ever thought that the topic of social class sounded abstract or dry – or that it was barely relevant to the education of psychologists – this is the text for you. Anne Noonan and William Ming Liu have created a psychological perspective on social class that is comprehensive, scholarly, and politically-literate, but also accessible, spirited, personal, and contemporary. Students and other readers will find engaging essays and exercises throughout the book that invite them into the exploration as they see its connections to other social justice issues and to their development as psychologists and counselors. Highly recommended.'

Laura Smith, *Teachers College, Columbia University, USA*

'Reading this wonderful book feels like you are in a conversation with the authors in their living rooms. This book is infused with warmth, intellectual rigor, fascinating narratives, and a call for readers to fully engage in the complex world of social class. The book will inspire many students who will resonate with the content and also will find their life stories represented in the narratives and text. In addition, the authors provided a very insightful perspective on the intersectionality of social identities, creating conceptual connections that are innovative and transformative. I strongly recommend this book for students, instructors, scholars, and interested readers who would like to engage with authors who share themselves and their fascinating ideas with compassion and creativity.'

David L. Blustein, *Boston College, USA*

Psychology and the Social Class Worldview

This unique textbook explores the complex topic of social class, explaining the many psychological nuances of class and classism in people's lives as subjective and phenomenological experiences.

Social class can be a deeply personal, complicated topic that is often frustrating and uncomfortable to discuss, and as such has often been a blind spot in teaching and academic literature. For the first time, Noonan and Liu look to address this in one comprehensive text, using a combination of first-person narratives, academic approaches to class, and psychology's contributions to the subject. Across seven chapters, the book introduces a highly accessible theoretical model of the psychology of social class, Liu's own Social Class Worldview Model. Using vivid autobiographical texts to bring the theoretical model to life, the authors show how our worldviews develop through interactions with our social class and economic environment and provide a unique array of methods and skill sets to help incorporate the model into teaching. Each section of the book guides the reader through core concepts in the area, from socioeconomic factors, social structures, poverty, race, racism, White privilege, and White supremacy.

Featuring activity suggestions, discussion questions, and writing prompts to help apply theory to real-life narratives, this is the ideal resource for students and instructors across psychology, sociology, health economics, and social work, as well as anyone taking courses on examining social class.

Anne E. Noonan is Professor of Psychology at Salem State University, Massachusetts, USA, where she regularly teaches courses in the writing-intensive curriculum, as well as in the diversity, power dynamics, and social justice curriculum. She is also a published author of creative nonfiction. Her research interests include the psychology of interpersonal relationships, the psychological and subjective aspects of social class and other social constructs, and narrative psychology.

William Ming Liu is Professor of Counseling Psychology and Department Chair at the University of Maryland, USA. He is the author or editor of several books on social class in the helping professions, Asian American men and masculinities, and multicultural competencies in counseling. His research interests are in social class and classisms, men and masculinity, and White supremacy and White privileges.

Psychology and the Social Class Worldview

A Narrative-Based Introduction

Anne E. Noonan and William Ming Liu

Routledge
Taylor & Francis Group

LONDON AND NEW YORK

Cover image: © Kumiko Shimizu/EyeEm/Getty Images

First published 2022
by Routledge
2 Park Square, Milton Park, Abingdon, Oxon OX14 4RN

and by Routledge
605 Third Avenue, New York, NY 10158

Routledge is an imprint of the Taylor & Francis Group, an informa business

British Library Cataloguing-in-Publication Data
A catalogue record for this book is available from the British Library

Library of Congress Cataloging-in-Publication Data
Names: Noonan, Anne E., author. | Liu, William Ming, author.
Title: Psychology and social class worldview : a narrative-based introduction /
    Anne E. Noonan and William Ming Liu.
Description: Abingdon, Oxon ; New York, NY : Routledge, 2022. | Includes bibliographical
    references and index. |
Identifiers: LCCN 2021031491 (print) | LCCN 2021031492 (ebook) | ISBN 9780367322601
    (paperback) | ISBN 9780367322618 (hardback) | ISBN 9780429317606 (ebook)
Subjects: LCSH: Social classes—Psychological aspects.
Classification: LCC HT609 .N66 2022 (print) | LCC HT609 (ebook) | DDC 305.501/9—dc23
LC record available at https://lccn.loc.gov/2021031491
LC ebook record available at https://lccn.loc.gov/2021031492

ISBN: 978-0-367-32261-8 (hbk)
ISBN: 978-0-367-32260-1 (pbk)
ISBN: 978-0-429-31760-6 (ebk)

DOI: 10.4324/9780429317606

Typeset in Bembo
by Apex CoVantage, LLC

Access the Support Material: www.routledge.com/9780367322601

AEN: To my PSY 344 students: Past, present, and future

WML: To Rossina, Bella Rose, Judy, Aurora, Raphael, Robert, and to my PoPo

Contents

Figures

Tables

Acknowledgments

"The Poet and The Pauper" by Meliza Bañales. Published in *Without a Net: The Female Experience of Growing Up Working Class*, 2003, edited by Michelle Tea. Copyright 2003 by Seal/Avalon/Hatchette. Reprinted by permission of Meliza Bañales.

"Thanks, But No Thanks" by Courtney Eldridge; from ALONE IN THE KITCHEN WITH AN EGGPLANT edited by Jenni Ferrari-Adler, copyright © 2007 by Jenni Ferrari-Adler. Used by permission of Riverhead, an imprint of Penguin Publishing Group, a division of Penguin Random House LLC. All rights reserved.

"Ghetto Fabulous" by Tina Fakhrid-Deen. Published in *Without a Net: The Female Experience of Growing Up Working Class*, 2003, edited by Michelle Tea. Copyright 2003 by Seal/Avalon/Hatchette. Reprinted by permission of Tina Fakhrid-Deen.

"Winter Coat" by Terri Griffith. Published in *Without a Net: The Female Experience of Growing Up Working Class*, 2003, edited by Michelle Tea. Copyright © 2003 by Seal/Avalon/Hatchette. Reprinted by permission of Terri Griffith.

Excerpt(s) from ON THE ROAD by Jack Kerouac, copyright © 1955, 1957, by John Sampas, Literary Representative, the Estate of Stella Sampas Kerouac; John Lash, Executor of the Estate of Jan Kerouac; Nancy Bump; and Anthony M. Sampas. Used by permission of Viking Books, an imprint of Penguin Publishing Group, a division of Penguin Random House LLC. All rights reserved.

"The Breadwinner" by William M. Liu. A version of this essay was delivered at the conference *Counseling Men in Difficult Times: Strategies for the Mental Health Needs of Men*, April 2010, California State University. Copyright 2010 by William M. Liu. Reprinted by permission of William M. Liu.

"Stink Tree" by Anne Noonan. Published in *Longridge Review*, Fall 2018. Copyright 2018 by Anne Noonan. Reprinted by permission of Anne Noonan.

"A Good School" by J.D. Scrimgeour. Published in *Themes for English B: A Professor's Education In and Out of Class* by University of Georgia Press. Copyright © 2006 by John David Scrimgeour. Reprinted by permission of J.D. Scrimgeour.

AEN: Thank you to Michael Mobley for introducing me to Will Liu. Thank you to Deborah Belle for suggesting, over coffee in Cambridge, that it can be liberating to begin writing a book in the middle rather than at the beginning. Thank you to the writers who gave personal permission for us to include their work: Meliza Bañales, Tina Fakhrid-Deen, Terri Griffith, and J.D. Scrimgeour. Our email conversations were so uplifting. Thank you to Nancy Marshall for the phrase "intellectual playdate" referenced in Chapter 2. And thank you to Virginia Martinez for allowing me to begin this book with the *bougie* story.

WML: I want to express my gratitude to Anne E. Noonan for including me in this extraordinary project. This book project would not have been completed without Anne's encouragement and support as I navigated moving to a new state and starting a new job. I also want to thank Michael Mobley for introducing me to Anne and this book project.

Introduction
The power of story

We, the authors of this textbook, want to tell you four stories. Bear with us: we promise that this book is not about us. Really. To prove that point, we'll make it about you right now. Before you do anything else – and without looking anything up – write down a definition of social class. Try to make it as formal and complete as you can.

And now that you've done that, here are four brief stories from our lives.

Story 1 (Anne E. Noonan): A few weeks ago a student called me *bougie* because of the salad I was eating when she stopped by my office. Do you know the word? Perhaps you know the word by another spelling (bougee, boujee, boujee, or boujie). Definitions of this adjective also vary, ranging from middle class, to trying to appear wealthier than one really is, to snobby and out of touch. Let me be clear. I don't believe the student, who identifies as Latinx, meant to offend me, her White, middle-aged professor. She has confirmed this. She was speaking humorously and playfully, having learned about my weakness for students with a sense of humor and a tendency to challenge the status quo. And to be fair, I *was* eating a salad of leafy greens, quinoa, dried cranberries, and pepitas. And I *was* eating that salad out of a mason jar.

What Do You Think?: If you know the term *bougie*, when did you first hear it, and in what context? How would you define it? Why did I mention the student's and my own race/ethnicity? Does that matter? And what about my salad? Does what I eat for lunch have anything to do with the topic of this book: the psychology of social class? Do you know what a mason jar is, and, if so, does it actually mean anything that someone is eating from one? Finally – and perhaps the most important question of all – scholars of linguistics tell us that words exist for a reason, so it must be the case that *bougie* exists for a reason (Brown, 2006). What is that reason? Why do we need a word for people whom we think are pretending to be wealthier than they really are?

Story 2 (William Ming Liu): When I was a newly minted assistant professor, I was at a conference and among a number of distinguished faculty, many of whom I admired for their scholarship on social justice and anti-racism. At the time, I was just starting to publish my work on social class and was getting some recognition for this research. During dinner, I had just started to put food into my mouth when one of the professors asked me about my thoughts about *White trash*. My thoughts raced, and I felt a bit panicked inside but tried to muster as much calm as possible. In order to buy myself some time to respond, I chewed really slowly, inflated my cheeks a bit to make it look like I had too much food in my mouth, and pointed to my mouth to

DOI: 10.4324/9780429317606-1

show them I was chewing. *How do I answer this question without destroying my nascent career?* The questioner was intentional and unapologetic about using this term to describe a particular group of White people, and since I was the *social class guy*, they were asking this as a serious question about Whiteness and poverty.[1]

What Do You Think?: Do you ever use the terms *White trash, hillbilly*, or *redneck*? If so, when and under what conditions? When did you first come to understand what these terms meant? What do we intend when we use these words; that is, what are we trying to accomplish with them? For some White people, being called White trash can certainly be hurtful and perhaps even trauma-inducing, in that trashy typically means lazy, dirty, violent, or impoverished. But for other White people, the term White trash points to an identity to embrace. How did these two possibilities (pain and pride) emerge? To take this even further, why does the word "White" precede the word "trash"? Why is that specifier there, and why does that distinction need to be made? Some scholars believe that, in addition to the inherent classism of "White trash," the term is inherently racist in that it suggests that White people aren't usually poor, lazy, dirty, or violent, unlike people who are Black, Indigenous, Latinx, Asian, or Other People of Color. What do you think of that suggestion?

Story 3 (Anne again): The context in which a student called me *bougie* was my workplace: a mid-sized public university north of Boston. I attended an undergraduate institution within this same state system and then went to graduate school at a more prestigious private university in Boston. After earning my doctoral degree, I worked as a research scientist at a for-profit health research organization, and then at an elite, private women's college west of Boston. These different contexts held a different social class meaning for me, and as I look back on these years, I see that my levels of comfort and awareness about social class differed in each place. In college, I didn't think much about the prestige of a public college vs. a more elite private college, other than having heard and used the term "a really good school" back in high school, when my friends and I discussed college admissions. (The college I attended was not called a "really good school.") But in the early days of graduate school, I felt slightly less respected than my fellow students who came from Yale or Harvard or a place of which I had never heard – Pomona College. And at the elite, private college where I worked, I felt rather out of step with the wealthy donors and alumnae with whom I interacted to raise funding for, and awareness of, the research my colleagues and I were conducting.

What Do You Think?: Have you felt different social class meanings in the various contexts in which you've operated? If you're reading this book as a college student, is the college you attend considered relatively prestigious or relatively less prestigious? That is, aside from whether you think your institution is a "good school," do others think that it is? Have you found that in certain times of your life or in certain contexts, you are more or less aware of who you are in terms of social class or who other people are in terms of social class? Or have you felt more or less comfortable in different contexts because of your social class?

---

1   Throughout this book, we intentionally use "they" and "them" as singular, as well as plural pronouns. This choice is consistent with the style and grammar guidelines of the American Psychological Association, specifically the guideline to "use 'they' as a generic third-person singular pronoun to refer to a person whose gender is unknown or irrelevant to the context of the usage." For more information, see apastyle.apa.org.

Story 4 (Will again): When we moved from Los Angeles to Iowa, my wife and I bought our first house. We were able to buy a house through the collective financial support of our families, a bank that deemed a professorship a stable job, and one that considered two cis–het (cisgender and heterosexual) Asian Americans as qualified loan applicants. One evening, as we were walking around our neighborhood, I had a growing uneasiness. In the neighborhood we'd moved into, it was customary for people to leave their garage doors open. I wasn't sure why they did this. Weren't they afraid that the things in their garage would be stolen or that someone would just walk into their garage and straight into their house? My neighbors never seemed to share those worries.

Open garage doors, as we came to understand, were a way to show others that you're home and that neighbors are welcome to come by. We, of course, didn't realize this until we started to get "drop-ins" from our neighbors. What I appreciated about our neighbors was their willingness to lend out their lawnmowers, hedge trimmers, and even their garden hoses. Having just relocated from our apartment on Sunset Boulevard in West Hollywood, we had never really thought about what it meant to have a house – in a neighborhood – surrounded by people who cared deeply about their homes, their driveways, and their lawns. Their offerings, I came to understand, were subtle reminders that there were certain expectations of us as homeowners in that community. Up to that point, we had no idea how many different options there are for lawnmowers. But we learned.

What Do You Think?: How does moving from one place to another influence the ways we behave (e.g., the clothing we wear, the way we speak)? How do we learn there are new rules in new places? Have you ever had the experience of being new to a context and receiving subtle, or not so subtle, lessons about what is expected? Have you yourself ever communicated such messages to newcomers in your neighborhood or in some other context? What was it like to either adjust and accommodate the new environment or try to resist "fitting in?"

★★★

These are four stories from our lives. Our stories are not earth-shattering, epic tales worthy of biographical (or perhaps even autobiographical) attention. They are not unique, special stories told by singularly compelling individuals. As a cisgender White woman and a cisgender Asian American man, our stories about social class will undoubtedly overlap with stories about how we experience race, gender, and perhaps other social categories, such as age, sexual orientation, ability status, gender identity, religion, and . . . well, the list could go on and on.

At this point, you may be thinking, "Wait. What is social class anyway? How are we defining that term?" If so, good for you, because definitions are always important. At the beginning of this chapter, we asked you to develop your own definition of social class. Because we both have asked our students over the years to perform the same task, we're pretty confident that your definition is excellent. But we also would hazard a guess that your definition may have left out some important pieces.

Let us offer you four different definitions of social class. We do this not to annoy or confuse you, but rather to demonstrate two things. The first is that social class is an inherently complicated phenomenon. The second is that experts in the disciplines that study social class do not always agree on definitions.

Perhaps the simplest definition we've seen of social class was provided in a collection of newspaper articles (Correspondents of the New York Times, 2005): "classes are groups of people of similar economic and social position." A leading sociology textbook defines social class as "a group of people with shared life chances, economic opportunities, and lifestyle" (Stuber, 2016). A group of psychologists offers this definition: "an individual or group's relative position in an economic–social–cultural hierarchy" in which "power, prestige, and control over resources" are central concerns (Diemer et al., 2013). And Will, in previous scholarship in the area (Liu, 2011), has taken even more complexity into account in the following.

> A class is an economic group within which an individual belongs, and the individual perceives material (i.e., types of belongings, neighborhood) and non-material (i.e., educational level) boundaries. The individual may observe other "classes" which are perceived to be, in subjective hierarchy, higher, lower, and at the same place (i.e., lateral) as the individual's own class. . . . Each class is perceived to have its own culture, and the further away the social class group is . . . the more unfamiliar the culture is.

The first definition comes from journalists, the second comes from a sociologist, the third comes from a group of psychologists, and the fourth comes from Will, a counseling psychologist. Political scientists, of course, would have a different definition and perspective, as would social justice scholars, historians, economists, or specialists in labor studies or workforce development. As different as these definitions might be, we imagine that you see some areas of similarity and overlap in them. What you also may have noticed is that the definitions as we present them progress from one focusing mainly on external or structural factors ("groups," "position"), to ones that incorporate a whole web of phenomena, represented by words such as opportunities, lifestyle, power, prestige, control, boundaries, a sense of positionality (being higher or lower than others), as well as cultural familiarity.

Wow, right? It's a lot. So perhaps a simpler formulation will be most helpful at this point. In this book, we certainly pay attention to how economic opportunity and economic experience are set up, but we're most interested in the more *subjective* aspects of social class – that is, in how social structures impact individual lives and how people internalize those external structures. We're interested in how people experience social class in their everyday lives, and in how they experience and enact different forms of classism, which we'll refer to as *classisms*.[2]

As we've suggested previously, we're also concerned with how our experiences with social class and classisms intersect with our experiences of race, gender, and other forms of identity/social group membership. You may have noticed previously that when we mentioned our racial identities, we capitalized both "Asian American" and "White." There is ongoing debate in psychology and elsewhere about whether to capitalize race-related terms in general; whether, more specifically, to capitalize or minimize the term "White"; and which acronym (e.g. POC, BIPOC, POCI) for People of Color is most

---

2   We'll devote Chapters 5 and 6 to the topic of classisms, but for those wishing an earlier definition, the Social Class Worldview Model-Revised defines classism as "a behavior acted on others, an experience of discrimination to the self, and an internalized dissonance that occurs when an individual perceives [themselves] to be out of accord with others" (Liu, 2011, p. 179).

inclusive of their lived experience. Here, we've made the decision to use the phrase Black, Indigenous, and Other People of Color (major words capitalized) and its acronym BIPOC. We've also decided to present the word "White" in its upper-case form. While we agree with scholars that Whiteness needs to be decentered and de-emphasized in order to bring other racial identities/social group memberships into the foreground, we take the lead from those choosing to capitalize the word to highlight Whiteness as a specific racial identity with a particular history, rather than the default category of, as historian Nell Irwin Painter puts it, "unraced individuality" (Painter, 2020).

And now let's return to that notion of stories about social class. The two of us began this introduction with two stories each from our lives, and we could have told more. No doubt you could tell many of your own stories about social class. We all can. You'll notice that this textbook provides first-person nonfiction essays written by people from a variety of walks of life (including one from each of us).[3] An exception to this is in the next chapter, in which we use a fictional excerpt. Creative nonfiction essays are, of course, just one source of stories about people's lives. In Will's role as a counseling psychologist, he has heard many social class stories told by clients over the years, and Anne has heard numerous stories as an interview-based qualitative researcher. Similarly, in our combined 30 years of teaching, both of us have heard countless stories from our students.

We have discovered over the years that when students read or hear the stories people tell about social class, they are much more open to thinking about social class in their own lives, and much less eager to say, for example, that "where you come from doesn't matter. It's only who you are as a person, on the inside, that matters." We don't think there's a psychologist out there who would argue that "who people are on the inside" doesn't matter. Of course, it matters. Our argument here is that "where we come from" and the meaning we make of that phrase, and of social class in general, are also hugely important.

And we hope to convince you of that in the following pages.

Discussion questions and assignment prompts

1   What's Your Story? Choose any of the following to write about.

> The meaning of social class and the different social classes is often taught in the family. Describe a story about a few lessons you have learned.
>
> What would your family members say about classism? Do you have examples of you or members of your family engaging in classism?
>
> How do you tell others about your social class without actually saying the words *social class*? That is, what words and phrases do you use?

References

Brown, D.W. (2006). Girls and guys, ghetto and bougie: Metapragmatics, ideology and the management of social identities. *Journal of Sociolinguistics*, *10*(5), 596–610.

---

3 More formally, we include essays in the genre known as creative nonfiction, which uses "the techniques [that] fiction writers, playwrights, and poets employ to present nonfiction – factually accurate prose about real people and events – in a compelling, vivid, dramatic manner: "www.creativenonfiction.org/online-reading/what-creative-nonfiction."

Correspondents of the New York Times. (2005). *Class matters*. New York, NY: Times Books.

Diemer, M.A., Mistry, R.S., Wadsworth, M.E., Lopez, I., & Reimers, F. (2013). Best practices in conceptualizing and measuring social class in psychological research. *Analyses of Social Issues and Public Policy*, *13*(1), 77–113. https://doi.org/10.1111/asap.12001

Liu, W.M. (2011). *Social class and classism in the helping professions: Research, theory, and practice*. Thousand Oaks, CA: Sage Publications.

Painter, N.I. (2020, July 22). Why "White" should be capitalized, too. *Washington Post*. www.washingtonpost.com/opinions/2020/07/22/why-white-should-be-capitalized/

Stuber, J. (2016). *Exploring inequality: A sociological approach*. New York, NY: Oxford University Press.

1 Social class

It's complicated

Check your comprehension

- Multiple definitions of social class exist, ranging from quite simple ones to more complicated versions that include phenomena such as beliefs and perceptions, boundaries, sense of belonging, status ordering, and culture.
- This book focuses on people's subjective understandings of social class and their lived experience of social class and classisms.
- We all have social class stories to tell and engaging with stories is an excellent way to understand the many nuances of social class. Thus, this book includes a collection of personal (creative nonfiction) essays from various authors.

What do you think?

1 Without looking anything up, what social class are you in? If it's easier to think about this in terms of your family of origin, in what social class is your family?
2 Many people answer this first question by saying "it's complicated." If social class is complicated for you/your family in any way, write a few sentences about why and how that is true.
3 How many social classes are there? List them, and if you think there's an order, list them in order.

Engage with a narrative and find social class markers

Instead of the usual nonfiction essays we will share in this book, what follows is an excerpt from the world of fiction: Jack Kerouac's 1957 novel about the Beat Generation, *On the Road*. Underline, circle, or take notes on every word or phrase that puts the idea of social class into your mind or signals to you that social class is operating. It may help to think of these as "social class markers." We'll revisit your work later in the chapter.

Box 1.1: Excerpt – *On the Road* by Jack Kerouac

The last time I saw him it was under strange and sad circumstances. Henri Cri had arrived in New York after having gone round the world several times in ships. I wanted him to meet and know Neal. They did meet but Neal couldn't talk any

---

DOI: 10.4324/9780429317606-2

more and said nothing, and Henri turned away. Henri had gotten tickets for the Duke Ellington concert at the Metropolitan Opera and insisted Joan and I come with him and his girl. Henri was fat and sad but still the eager and formal gentleman and he wanted to do things the right way as he emphasized. So he got his bookie to drive us to the concert in a Cadillac. It was a cold winter night. The Cadillac was parked and ready to go. Neal stood outside the windows with his bags ready to go to Penn Station and on across the land. "Goodbye Neal" I said. "I sure wish I didn't have to go to the concert." "D'you think I can ride to 40th St. with you?" he whispered. "Want to be with you as much as possible, m'boy and besides it's so durned cold in this here New Yawk . . ." I whispered to Henri. No, he wouldn't have it, he liked me but he didn't like my friends. I wasn't going to start all over again ruining his planned evenings as I had done at Alfred's in San Francisco in 1947 with Allan Temko. "Absolutely out of the question Jack!" Poor Henri, he had a special necktie made for this evening; on it was painted a replica of the concert tickets, and the names Jack and Joan and Henri and Vicki, the girl, together with a series of sad jokes and some of his favorite sayings such as "You can't teach the old maestro a new tune." So Neal couldn't ride uptown with us and the only thing I could do was sit in the back of the Cadillac and wave at him. The bookie at the wheel also wanted nothing to do with Neal. Neal, ragged in a motheaten overcoat he brought specially for the freezing temperatures of the East, walked off alone and the last I saw of him he rounded the corner of 7th Ave., eyes on the street ahead, and bent to it again. Poor little Joan my wife to whom I'd told everything about Neal began almost to cry. "Oh we shouldn't let him go like this. What'll we do?" Old Neal's gone I thought, and out loud I said, "He'll be all right."

Into which social class do I fit?

This chapter has the word "complicated" in the title, and you'll recall that in the introductory chapter, we shared four different definitions of social class with you. Considering that scholars (even those in the same discipline) don't always agree on what social class is or how to define it, you may have had some difficulty answering the questions at the beginning of this chapter. In our university classrooms, when we share this initial complexity with students, they sometimes ask in frustration, "If it's that complicated, how can I ever know what social class I'm in?" And we have to admit it: fair point.

So, let's start where most people begin thinking about social class: money. Look back at the definition of social class that you wrote while reading the introductory chapter. Did money make an appearance, or did the word "financial," or "economic," or "resources"? Those words probably did. In fact, we can't imagine thinking about social class without the inclusion of some of those words, and you'll notice they appear in some form in all of the definitions we shared.

But an interesting aspect of theories and definitions of social class is an agreement that while money or economic/financial resources matter, social class is about a whole lot more than money. And even if social class really was just about money, as Will points out in previous work (Liu, 2011), the idea of "money" is itself fairly complicated. "Money" might mean annual salaries, hourly wages from employment, or income from other sources. The word also might refer to inherited wealth or accumulated wealth, with wealth defined simply as what one owns minus what one owes. Each of these different interpretations of money can impact the way we see ourselves and how we relate to other people, and this impact becomes even more profound when we take a person's race and ethnicity into account. Money can also be treated more symbolically, especially as our society increasingly relies upon electronic means of receiving, transferring, or exchanging funds. And what about financial anxiety, credit card debt, and student loans? Where do those fit into our ideas about money?

For decades, the social sciences have categorized people into different social classes via a construct with which you may be familiar: socioeconomic status (SES). This construct includes the idea of money, but as Diemer and colleagues (2013) remind us, it also extends to "relatively objective indicators of power, prestige, and control over resources, such as income, wealth, educational level, and occupational prestige" (Diemer et al., 2013, p. 79). Notice the word *objective* in Diemer et al.'s definition, a term which suggests that the components of SES are quantifiable and easily categorized.

Quantification in the realm of social class simply means that more of some quantity can be represented as higher in some index or category. But what does "higher" actually mean when it comes to someone's job? To answer that question, researchers have created prestige indices for occupations – that is, a hierarchy of jobs based on whether people see that job as prestigious (such as a banker) or less prestigious[1] (such as a plumber). These measures typically are based on what people, in general, think about traditional types of occupations and the education levels and skills required for them. It should be noted here that these hierarchies tend to be developed from the opinions, perceptions, and experiences of people in prestigious jobs, and therefore not everyone gets to participate in ranking these jobs.

Another problem, of course, is that these prestige measures may not be able to keep up with the rapidly expanding digital nature of our culture. For instance, consider a social media influencer who is paid – sometimes in the millions of dollars – according to the number of followers they attract on a given platform rather than on the basis of educational level or their ability to create a product. How would the occupation of influencer be rated using traditional measures of prestige? Similarly, researchers may be showing a built-in bias when they assume that all people want higher levels of education, more money, and more upward mobility, but as will be discussed later, this is not always the case.

Scholars have pointed to additional ways that the SES construct fails to capture all the psychological complexity of social class. For example, Lott (2012) tells us that the idea of "class" certainly includes the components of SES but also transcends SES, incorporating phenomena such as "status, expectations, location, and power, as defined by access to resources" (p. 650). Further, as Will pointed out in previous work, "Once you categorize someone [into a social class group], there is no discussion of how the person entered the group, exists in that group, and stays in that group" (Liu, 2011, p. 13). Given these additional considerations of phenomena, such as status and power, a focus solely on SES may obscure the powerful ways that social class intersects with race, gender, and other forms

---

1   Ironically, the *Oxford English Dictionary* tells us that the original meaning of *prestige* (from French and Latin) refers to an illusion or trick, and antonyms included esteem, honor, and respectability.

of social identities/social constructs, a topic to which we'll repeatedly turn in subsequent chapters.[2]

Objective measures of SES also cannot help us understand the web of belief systems that we develop with regard to matters such as fairness, effort, and meritocracy. For example, people might think that the distribution (i.e., the spread) of economic social classes reflects how much effort we put into work, school, or saving money. Meritocracy can be seen as a kind of social agreement that people *should be* rewarded for hard work, effort, and good financial decisions, and people *should not* cheat the system, "cut in line," or change the rules. Stated more simply, meritocracy suggests that people are in the social class they're in because they deserve to be, and anyone dissatisfied with their current social class can certainly find a better job or pursue a higher level of education. (Will discusses meritocracy in more depth in Chapter 6.)

In addition to describing objective measures of social class, Diemer and colleagues (2013) also point to more *subjective* ways of examining social class, and they highlight two main approaches: the Social Class Worldview Model-Revised (SCWM-R; the subject of this book) and the Subjective Social Status approach developed by psychologist Nancy Adler and colleagues (Adler et al., 2000). Subjective Social Status is assessed by having research participants engage with an image of a ladder bearing ten rungs (Figure 1.1). Read the instructions provided and see how you would mark up the ladder.

How easy or difficult was it for you to find the "correct" rung for you or your family? Anne once shared the ladder tool in a presentation at her former workplace, a research center of a prestigious liberal arts college in Massachusetts. The presentation was for the center's Board of Directors, whom one might assume would occupy the upper rungs of the ladder and be able to complete the task easily. But Anne heard actual *groaning* as people tried to find the correct rung on the ladder. The reason for this difficulty, which you may have already discovered on your own, is that one might be on a high rung in terms of income but on a lower rung in terms of occupation or a middle rung in terms of education level. So how does one average those out and come up with the correct rung? And how does one take race into account when working with the ladder tool? We agree that it's complicated, and we'll return to this tool in Chapter 3.

How many social classes are there?

One of the "What Do You Think?" questions at the beginning of this chapter asked you to name some different social classes, and we're confident that you were able to list more than one. You may also have put those groupings or classes into some sort of order, with groups ranking higher or lower. Indeed, most formulations of social class involve such layers or *strata*. Stuber (2016) explains that a typical model of social class assumes a pyramid shape of various layers, with a pattern of more people near or at the bottom of the pyramid than at the top.

But how many layers or classes are there? Well – and this answer won't surprise you – it depends. There are many ways to answer this question that make sense, but we'll mention just a few here. Lott (2012) makes reference to three: working class, middle class, and a

---

2   Throughout the book, we use the phrase social identities/social constructs to refer to the interrelated matters of identifying ourselves, how we are identified by others, and the ways that the culture assigns meaning to identity (social constructs).

wealthy class. Stuber suggests five (an underclass, a working class, middle class, upper middle, and upper class). Of course, the original social class theorist Karl Marx asserted only two: owners and workers. Over the years, our students have appreciated the four groupings suggested by Smith (2010). See if you can more easily place yourself/your family into one of these categories.

- *Poverty: Predominantly describes working-class people who, because of unemployment, low-wage jobs, health problems, or other crises are without enough income to support their families' basic needs.*
- *Working class: People who have little power or authority in the workplace, little control over the availability or content of jobs, and little say in the decisions that affect their access to health care, education, and housing. They tend to have lower levels of income, net worth, and formal education than more powerful classes.*
- *Middle class: Professionals, managers, small business owners, often college-educated and salaried. Middle-class people have more autonomy and control in the workplace than working-class people, and more economic security; however, they rely upon earnings from work to support themselves.*
- *Owning class: People who own enough wealth and property that they do not need to work to support themselves (although they may choose to); people who own and control the resources by which other people earn a living. The owning class includes people who, as a result of their economic power, also have significant social, cultural, and political power relative to other classes.*

It's important to note that Smith's framework doesn't limit us to just four groups if we believe that further gradation might make sense. She suggests, for example, that "middle class" may include an upper middle class; other scholars have suggested a lower middle class as well. Smith also suggests that the "poverty" class might include people thought of as "the working poor," and psychologists have more recently emphasized the profound implications for those living in what has been called deep poverty (Davis & Williams, 2020).

Using "and" instead of "vs.": the individual/structural distinction

If you were to ask a random person on the street about the difference between sociology and psychology, you might hear a response that psychology concerns itself with people, while sociology concerns itself with social structures, or with how society is set up. While this distinction is somewhat accurate, the truth is . . . you guessed it . . . a bit more complicated.

If you have studied sociology, you may recall that field being defined as the systematic study of human society, and of course, there is ample attention to structural factors. Breezing through the table of contents in any introductory textbook will show you key terms such as social stratification – that idea of layers, or strata – and social structures, which exist at larger-scale macro-levels and smaller-scale micro-levels. Yet you will also see ample attention to individual factors, with terms such as social status, social identity, and people's position (or *positionalities*) in social structures. For the most part, sociologists take these larger structural forces as their starting point and then infer how these forces impact the individual. As Stuber (2016) puts it, in examining the "game of life," sociology cares about "the game" itself – that is, more macro-level (or structural) forces – but also cares about individual "players" in the game.

Similarly, you may recall introductory psychology definitions of psychology as the scientific study of behavior and mental processes (affect/emotion and cognition), which certainly sounds focused on individuals. However, modern conceptualizations, theories, and research in psychology care a great deal about cultural and structural factors, as exemplified by the subdiscipline of social psychology, scholarship in the area of multicultural competencies (Sue et al., 1992), and racial identity (Helms, 2007, 2020) or by the commitment of counseling psychologists to examine race and culture (e.g., Neville & Carter, 2005) and – more recently – anti-Black racism and Black survival and wellness (Academics for Black Survival and Wellness, 2021; Mosley et al., 2020). Other examples include the "sociocultural selves" perspective that sees individual and structural factors as "interdependent forces . . . best understood together" (Stephens et al., 2012), young people's increasingly "sociocentric" ways of thinking about economic circumstances (Flanagan & Tucker, 1999), and Bronfenbrenner's (2005) ecological model, which depicts individuals as nested within circles of influence ranging from close to the individual (e.g., family, school) to more distant from the individual (e.g., the national economy).

Therefore, this book will not draw rigid distinctions between these two academic disciplines, or between individual and structural factors. Sure, psychologists may sometimes need reminders that individuals don't have unlimited free will to create their worlds. And we would suggest that sociologists may sometimes need reminders that individuals internalize social structures and actively make sense of them in diverse ways that demand to be understood. But to make use of Stuber's words, let's assume that to understand anything worth understanding, both the "player" and the "game" matter. Or, as Stephens et al. (2012) remind us, these forces are best understood together.

Bringing the outside in: internalizing the structural

So, where does a *psychology* of social class fit into all of this complexity? In Chapter 2, we'll focus on how psychology has examined and is currently examining social class, some of that work looking at the "objective" SES indicators. But for the purposes of this chapter, recall that we are largely concerned in this book with the more *subjective* aspects of social class and classisms, and the *lived experience* of social class. In other words, we're most interested in how social structures "get inside." And we're interested in how individuals interact with one another vis-à-vis these structures and strata. Recall Will's assertion that important questions remain after people have placed themselves into a social class group. How did they get into that group? How do they exist in that group? And, whether they stay in that group or leave it, what does the staying or the leaving look like?

Look back at that Subjective Social Status Ladder in Figure 1.1, and imagine that you're actually standing on the rung where you placed your X. While standing on your rung, you would be able to see the rest of the ladder. For example, if you're not on the very bottom rung, you can look below you, and if you're not on the very upper rung, you can look above you. An important focus, then, for a *psychology* of social class, is how we see ourselves in relation to other people's positions on the ladder. Another appropriate focus is how we interact with people whom we consider to be "higher" or "lower" than we are. Interestingly, we also share our rungs with other people, so psychology is also operating when we interact with similar others. If we ground ourselves in the very definition of psychology, imagine all the behaviors and emotions and cognitions that surround this imaginary ladder. Might we act differently with people from whom we feel great distance on the ladder? Might we feel different emotions looking at people higher up than we are or lower? And what about cognition? How do we think about these matters, and how do we perceive differences and similarities? In short, how do we bring the outside in?

We wish to make an important point here. This book describes the SCWM-R, which is a *psychological* conceptualization of social class and classisms. The SCWM-R places a theoretical framework – a worldview and lens – around all of the "pieces" that make up

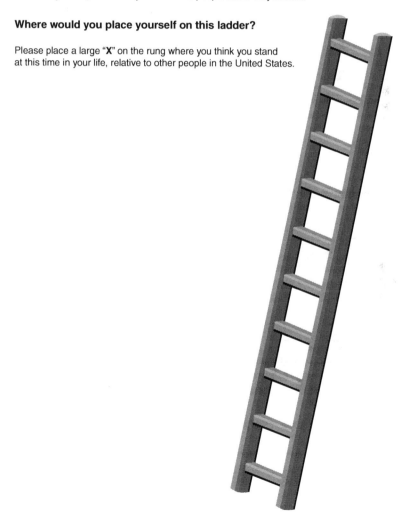

Think of this ladder as representing where people stand in the United States.

At the **top** of the ladder are the people who are the best off – those who have the most money, the most education and the most respected jobs. At the **bottom** are the people who are the worst off – who have the least money, least education, and the least respected jobs or no job. The higher up you are on this ladder, the closer you are to the people at the very top; the lower you are, the closer you are to the people at the very bottom.

Where would you place yourself on this ladder?

Please place a large "**X**" on the rung where you think you stand at this time in your life, relative to other people in the United States.

Figure 1.1: Subjective Social Status Ladder

Source: McArthur Research Network on SES and Health (https://macses.ucsf.edu/)

social class, as a way to help make sense of those pieces. For example, why do people, even in the same social class position, see and experience the world so differently? But we are in no way saying that economic inequalities, structural inequities, racism, or poverty are all about perception and are merely intrapsychic phenomena. That would be the opposite of what we are trying to convey. For example, in Chapter 3 we'll introduce the term Economic Cultures, which are real-life contexts and situations in which money, resources, and inequities have institutional, historical, and structural meanings.

Worldviews and blind spots

You know from the title of this book that a major area of focus here is the Social Class Worldview – that is, a way of coming to see how social class and classisms operate in the world and become a part of us. We'll have lots to say in the following chapters about how the worldview develops, but for now, it may be helpful to think about driving a car. When we drive, there is a field of vision incorporating what we can see, and there are blind spots or areas we cannot see without turning our heads or bodies. Coming to understand the psychology of social class involves examining one's own Social Class Worldview, and it also involves turning our heads, so to speak, to take in new phenomena and understandings.

Take the Kerouac excerpt as an example. How many words and phrases did you underline or circle? Over several years of a classroom exercise using this piece, students collectively have produced a compelling list of the many ways social class shows up in the reading. Yet no single student has individually generated such a complete list. One of the reasons might simply reflect the old saying in the corporate motivation world: "none of us is as smart as all of us." In other words, groups of people tend to know more than individual people know. Another reason may be the limitations inherent in our Social Class Worldviews, a topic to be discussed later in the book. By this we mean that even though we develop a way of seeing the world in terms of social class, that view is necessarily limited by the messages to which we're exposed and the various messengers in our lives.

By way of example, a student once remarked about the Kerouac excerpt that traveling on ships seemed to be a marker of social class in that such trips are usually expensive – a valid perspective. But another student replied that maybe the person on the ship was a worker rather than a passenger – also valid. The point here is that one student had "wealthy passenger" in their worldview, while another had "worker" in theirs. The different ways they had come to see ocean travel were valid but also had blind spots. However, by the end of class, everyone had both the wealthy-traveler perspective *and* the worker perspective in their Social Class Worldviews. Indeed, turning the head to see what we're not seeing can change up the worldview in important ways.

Another example of a blind spot comes from a formal dinner scene in the PBS television drama *Downton Abbey*. The elderly and aristocratic matriarch of the family, Violet Crawley (played by British actress Maggie Smith), hears someone say the word "weekend." Confused, she looks up and stammers, "What is a weekend?" Having never worked a day as a paid employee, the distinction between weekday and weekend was simply not in her worldview. One might also imagine someone holding down three jobs sarcastically asking that very same question, as might a person in a demanding professional position who regularly works 60+ hours a week, weekdays and weekends. The point is this. Each person might ask the same question but for very different reasons depending upon their respective worldviews and blind spots.

Which narratives matter?

Blind spots in the worldview are, of course, not limited to individuals who lack knowledge about social class and classisms. Many scholars have argued that the United States has cultural blind spots when it comes to social class, reflected in how we intentionally avoid social class–related topics or how our culture makes social class difficult to understand. We may know as a culture that social class matters, but we know this only to a point, and our knowledge is limited by a variety of forces. One force is the belief that, compared to England or India for example, the United States is a society without classes. A second force is the dominant achievement ideology in the United States: the meritocratic ideal that economic success is almost guaranteed if one works hard enough and is dedicated to success (Belle, 2006; Garrison et al., 2021). A third force is that people in the United States, when asked about social class, tend to say they're a member of the middle class, even if they occupy objectively lower or higher socioeconomic positions (Gallup, 2017). Fourth, because of cultural beliefs about the possibility of economic mobility, many people see themselves as *millionaires-to-be*, and social class problems such as inequalities and inequities are seen as irrelevant to their eventual wealth and power.

A fifth force is the belief that talking about social class is inappropriate or shows bad manners. Most people shy away from talking about social class because it means talking about money or bragging about status, and so *social class* can be rendered an unsafe or taboo topic within a family, between friends, and in our communities. Not surprisingly, many of us have little practice in talking about social class and classisms. Hence, sixth, even those Americans who may *want to* discuss matters of social class may have limited skill and experience doing so (Stuber, 2006) and can be, in fact, relatively "tongue-tied" (Noonan et al., 2007).

And finally, even when we do desire such conversation and maybe even possess some savvy, certain narratives (e.g., childhood poverty, lifestyles of the 1%, "rags to riches" mobility tales) tend to dominate the foreground. Important as these narratives are, they tend to relegate other narratives to the background or, worse, to blind spots in the visual field – that is, to blind spots in our worldviews. So, our cultural reluctance to talk about social class is worsened by our tendency to look at just a few aspects of social class (e.g., poverty, uber-wealthy celebrities). Thus, as a culture, we fail to draw a comprehensive portrait of how social class exists and shows up in the "real world."

A final word about complexity

If social class is a nuanced topic, further complexity comes from the fact that the general word "class" has numerous definitions. You already know that a class can simply be a group of people, or a group of objects, for example, as in a "best in class" designation for some product. The *Oxford English Dictionary* also defines class as an academic course (e.g., the class for which you are reading this textbook) and a student's year in school (e.g., the sophomore class). But consider also the uses of the word "class" that have more of an evaluative, or even judgmental, component: class as elegance, a person being a "class act," calling someone classy, or calling someone classless. Or think about Will Farrell's character in the *Anchorman* movies signing off with "Stay classy, San Diego," or the more sarcastic "stay classy" insult on social media and the many "keep it classy" fashion or decorating tips found online.

As you progress through this textbook, we ask that you keep an eye out for instances in which the discussion of social classes as groups of people veers into this evaluative or judgmental territory, and we urge you to pay attention to your emotional reactions to that shift. We suggest that any emotional reactions you have to the material in this book will provide valuable insights into your own Social Class Worldview.

Discussion questions/assignment prompts

1   Some people say they have never thought about social class or classism, and so starting to think about it is confusing, even anxiety provoking. If this scenario sounds familiar, discuss some reasons why you've been able to avoid thinking about your own social class.

2   What are the things that make up a wealthy person? What are the things that make up a middle-class person? Finally, what are the things that make up a poor person? By "things" here we mean possessions such as property and clothing but also manners, how people speak, how they get around (e.g., transportation), and what they are like in school or other contexts.

3   Intersectionality Check-In: When you imagined this wealthy person, poor person, and middle-class person, what race did you imagine them to be? What gender did you imagine? We would argue that these images that we carry around with us, even if stereotypical, help us psychologically make sense of social class and classisms. Why do you think you imagined the way you did? What might this tell you about your Social Class Worldview?

4   Digital Spotlight: If you spend time on social media, and using Smith's (2010) framework, which social classes do you see the most of, and which ones do you see represented less? Why do you think that is? Do some platforms (e.g., Instagram, TikTok) show more social class diversity than others? How do you make sense of that?

5   What's Your Story? Try to remember when you first became aware of social class differences. Perhaps this was an event or situation in which you felt different from a friend, a family member, or a neighbor. What did that feel like? How did you try to make sense of it? If you asked someone about these differences, what did they tell you?

References

Academics for Black Survival and Wellness. (2021). www.academics4blacklives.com/

Adler, N.E., Epel, E.S., Castellazzo, G., & Ickovics, J.R. (2000). Relationship of subjective and objective social status with psychological and physiological functioning: Preliminary data in healthy, White women. *Health Psychology, 19*(6), 86–592. https://doi.org/10.1037/0278-6133.19.6.586

Belle, D. (2006). Contested interpretations of economic inequality following Hurricane Katrina. *Analyses of Social Issues and Public Policy, 6*(1), 143–158. Publisher: Hoboken, NJ: Blackwell. https://doi.org/10.1111/j.1530-2415.2006.00111

Bronfenbrenner, U. (2005). *Making human beings human: Bioecological perspectives on human development.* Thousand Oaks, CA: Sage.

Davis, R.P., & Williams, W.R. (2020). Bringing psychologists to the fight against deep poverty. *American Psychologist, 75*(5), 655–667. https://doi.org/10.1037/amp0000650

Diemer, M.A., Mistry, R.S., Wadsworth, M.E., Lopez, I., & Reimers, F. (2013). Best practices in conceptualizing and measuring social class in psychological research. *Analyses of Social Issues and Public Policy, 13*(1), 77–113. https://doi.org/10.1111/asap.12001

Flanagan, C.A., & Tucker, C.J. (1999). Adolescents' explanations for political issues: Concordance with their views of self and society. *Developmental Psychology, 5*(5), 1198–1209. https://doi.org/10.1037/0012-1649.35.5.1198

Gallup. (2017). *Middle-class identification in U.S. at pre-recession levels.* https://news.gallup.com/poll/212660/middle-class-identification-pre-recession-levels.aspx

Garrison, Y.L., Rice, A., & Liu, W.M. (2021). The American meritocracy myth stress: Scale development and initial validation. *The Counseling Psychologist, 49*(1), 80–105. https://doi.org/10.1177/0011000020962072

Helms, J.E. (2007). Some better practices for measuring racial and ethnic identity constructs. *Journal of Counseling Psychology, 54*(3), 235–246. https://doi.org/10.1037/0022-0167.54.3.235

Helms, J.E. (2020). *A race is a nice thing to have: A guide to being a White person or understanding the White persons in your life* (3rd ed.). San Diego: Cognella.

Liu, W.M. (2011). *Social class and classism in the helping professions: Research, theory, and practice.* Thousand Oaks, CA: Sage Publications.

Lott, B. (2012). The social psychology of class and classism. *American Psychologist, 67,* 650–658. https://doi.org/10.1037/a0029369

Mosley, D., Hargons, C.N., Meiller, C., Angyal, B., Wheeler, P., Davis, C., & Stevens-Watkins, D. (2020). Critical consciousness of anti-Black racism: A practical model to prevent and resist racial trauma. *Journal of Counseling Psychology, 68*(1), 1–16. https://doi.org/10.1037/cou0000430

Neville, H., & Carter, R.T. (2005). Race and racism in counseling psychology research, training, and practice: A critical review, current trends, and future directions. *The Counseling Psychologist, 33*(4), 413–418. https://doi.org/10.1177/0011000005276733

Noonan, A.E., Hall, G., & Blustein, D. (2007). Urban adolescents' experience of social class in relationships at work. *Journal of Vocational Behavior, 70,* 542–560. https://doi.org/10.1016/j.jvb.2007.01.005

Smith, L. (2010). What is social class? In *Psychology, poverty, and the end of social exclusion: Putting our practice to work* (pp. 5–23). New York, NY: Teachers College Press.

Stephens, N.M., Marks, H.R., & Fryberg, S.A. (2012). Social class disparities in health and education: Reducing inequality by applying a sociocultural-self model of behavior. *Psychological Review, 119,* 723–744. https://doi.org/10.1037/a0029028

Stuber, J. (2006). Talk of class: The discursive repertoires of white working- and upper-middle-class college students. *Journal of Contemporary Ethnography, 5*(3), 285–318. https://doi.org/10.1177/0891241605283569

Stuber, J. (2016). *Exploring inequality: A sociological approach.* New York, NY: Oxford University Press.

Sue, D.W.; Arredondo, P., & McDavis, R.J. (1992). Multicultural competencies and standards: A call to the profession. *Journal of Multicultural Counseling and Development, 20*(2), 64–88.

2 What does a psychology of social class look like?

Internalizing the structural

Check your comprehension

- Psychologists and other social scientists have examined social class from objective and subjective perspectives.
- The academic study of social class involves a high level of complexity, and there are different answers to the question of how many social classes exist. One framework suggests four groups: poor, working class, middle class, and owning class.
- The psychology of social class is concerned with how people internalize external class structures or "bring the outside in."
- Individuals have blind spots in their Social Class Worldviews, and there are cultural blind spots as well that prevent us from seeing social class more comprehensively.

Engage with a narrative and find social class markers

In our combined 30 years of teaching about social class, we have found that students come to our classes with a wealth of knowledge about the psychological aspects of social class, even if they lack the terminology or awareness that they possess this knowledge. In Chapter 1, we asked you to identify anything that "looked like" social class in the excerpt from Kerouac's *On the Road*. For this chapter, we'll take that activity a bit deeper with an essay written by Will. Recall that psychology is defined as the scientific study of behavior and mental process, with mental processes broken down further into affect (emotions) and cognition (thoughts, memories, judgments). As you read Will's essay, make a note of any example of affect/emotion, behavior, and cognition that you think has *something to do with* social class, even if you can't articulate exactly why. Go with your gut and your instincts.

Box 2.1: Essay – "The Breadwinner" by William Ming Liu

The December before the shutdowns from the COVID pandemic, my father passed away. He was in another country, and his ashes lay there for me to visit one day. In writing this book about social class, I remembered this essay I presented at a conference about men and masculinity several years ago. In it, I wanted to talk about how classism, racism, and masculinity

---

DOI: 10.4324/9780429317606-3

created a toxic mix that was constantly inflected on my father's life, and consequentially in our family's life. Here is my essay.

Economic distress shuts men down.

But merely calling it distress diminishes the trauma and despondency of losing one's job and one's role as a breadwinner. Distress also doesn't capture the fact that men are, and have, over generations been coping and surviving under inequality. This intergenerational pattern of living under inequality has consequences both psychologically and physically, and the perniciousness of these effects is just as deleterious as living in a society that doesn't address racism.

We need to see distress as a symptom of social inequality which has occurred over multiple generations; it is societal classism, and it is systemic. Thus, focusing on individual effort and working hard is akin to asking someone faced with racism to ignore all the indicators of abuse and mistreatment and to just work hard; the responsibility then falls on those who are the targets of the injustice rather than those who perpetrate.

Working hard doesn't address the fact that quite simply there are just not enough jobs, and when there are jobs, they are not high paying ones. For many men and women, it means staying unemployed, or in part-time work and being underemployed.

As a psychologist, my interest is in understanding how men cope and survive in these contexts of economic downturns. I have learned that many men may rely on coping styles that they developed through repeated experiences with recessions and job-loss. They may also turn to ways of adapting they learned from their fathers. Many men may turn to these socialized ways of coping because many men may still be in the same or similar economic situation as their fathers.

What would it be like for a father to pass on the same struggles to his son; to watch his son suffer the ills of poverty, and to hope for something better but knowing that the drag of being poor impedes mobility?

It can be shameful for many men to be stuck and without any way out. How might these men adapt to the chronic anxiety, demoralization, and frustration?

For some men they may find problem ways to cope such as drinking, drugs, or sex. Other men are more self-destructive and violent.

Some men chose to leave.

~~

I'm not sure when I saw my father last. My father and I crossed by each other without saying much. What passed for conversation usually occurred on Post-it notes I left for him asking for some cash so I could put gas in my car. Every morning there was five or ten dollars on the table, which I took and left the house.

I remember once my father remarked that he didn't have enough money for a haircut. His circumstance was just one of many problems our family faced. Sometimes we didn't have the electricity on; sometimes our phone went out; sometimes we ate government cheese.

In our last apartment, a dark two-bedroom walk-up, the sunlight never seemed to make it past the living room, our dining room table was always in shadows. That is where my father sat and ate his meals. When I walked past him, he would always offer whatever he had. Sometimes I would take a bowl of soup but sit in front of the television.

Once he was done eating, he would leave for work and we would both continue on with our day.

In college, I chose to spend most of my nights at school. I hadn't given much thought to what my father was doing during his day. I assumed he went off to another cooking job. I knew he hated it, but I didn't ask. I didn't want to know; I'm not sure I could stand knowing how much he hated what he did. Most times I avoided looking at my father, but sometimes when I did, I'd see that his shoulders were more stooped and the color around his eyes had grown darker. He looked more tired; more worn-out; less like the father I remembered when I was younger.

Did he always look like that?

~~~

My father learned to live in silence. He was the product of three cultures – being Asian, a man, and someone who grew up poor. At one point he had made himself rich in Taiwan owning a propane distribution company. He had hoped to sell the business and use that money to create a better life for his family in America.

The money never came through. He always felt cheated out of the money. His family was in the United States, he had no money, and he had a wife and two boys. He turned to cooking --American food.

He never spoke much and he seemed to resist acculturating. Acculturating meant having American friends, socializing with Americans, and becoming an American man. Instead he chose us to translate and interact with everyone else.

We helped him save face and helped him be the man he had imagined himself. My father still imagined himself as the breadwinner.

~~~

Man as breadwinner is a strident expectation because of the strong mythology built around it. It has the sound of normalcy and permanence much like romantic love and marriage being the foundation of a civil society.

I suspect around those early campfires, the stories of farming were far less exciting than killing a boar, and so those stories became folklore and myth, and the single-male provider took root.

But as cities grew and societies became industrialized, and the division of labor became more entrenched, the roles of men and women became more equal – to the detriment of women. Women were excluded from workplaces and relegated to the domestic, and men were automatically assumed to be the head of the household until 1980.

Even though this visage of the breadwinner persists, economically, it is virtually impossible for a man to be the sole breadwinner. With stagnating wages for most high-school-educated men, it becomes almost impossible to be a single wage earner, work from 9-5, be home for dinner, and grill on the weekends. Many men have to work more and more to even have a chance of fulfilling the "breadwinner" role.

It seems that the only men who might be able to live out this role are the few who are wealthy. For them in the top 80th percentile, they have seen their incomes grow while the rest have seen their incomes drop.

For many other men, the conflict of trying to inhabit this role causes distress intra-psychically and interpersonally. During these economic downturns, these recessions or "man-cessions," partners and spouses may find themselves in a conflicting situation of being an equal provider but simultaneously colluding with the man's self-image and role as the breadwinner. Under the best economic situations these relationships are tenuous, and under duress, these relationships are bound for distress.

Economic distress is an acute situation, one that has been experienced repeatedly, and a problem with long roots. It is chronic and intergenerational. It is an emotional tone and a worldview that can be transmitted from father to son. At its foundation is the fear born of financial insecurity, transitory periods of poverty, and living and working in situations where there is little hope of escape from an endless cycle of unemployment, underemployment, and monotonous and arduous work.

For many men in these situations, their work is not a career. David Blustein's research suggests that many see it as merely a job; one of many manual and service jobs along a person's lifespan. Parents teach their children how to survive in these jobs; these are ways of making money, not personal discovery and self-actualization.

~~~

I hate fried chicken. My wife loves fried chicken. I can tell her the many reasons why I hate fried chicken but I can't seem to describe my relationship with that bird. I hate the smell of hot cooking oil. The grease of fried foods never comes off. Standing in front of a hot fryer I learned to deal with the sparks of oil that leap at you when you immerse cold wet chicken. After a while, I just stopped flinching and watched the chicken grow brown. *Mother.Fucking.Chicken.*

My parents owned a coffee shop. Two from what I remember. The one I worked in was the one we eventually sold—Lillie's Café. Lillie. Maybe because that sounded more American than Shu Shen or Nan Wen or Ming Yuan. Lillie.

On days I worked in the kitchen, I wore the same shirt, pants, and shoes. The grease started to make parts of my shirt see-thru. Those clothes smelled like the kitchen. Like food, but all food, nothing specific. And it smelled like sweat. Sometimes it got so hot, I'd stop wiping the sweat away and I just watch it drip. Years later, I saw a quote from George Orwell that said, ". . . the more one pays for food, the more sweat and spittle one is obliged to eat with it." I don't think Orwell ever saw the kitchen of an American coffee shop.

Every morning was prep time. Scramble eight dozen eggs.

Mix four tubs of pancake batter.

Chop and dice ham, onions, green peppers, red peppers, green chilies, and tomatoes.

Stock the bread for the toast.

Melt the butter and ready the oil.

Scoop the coffees into paper filters.

Regular coffee and decaf; two stacks ready for the morning rush.

~~~

Working in the restaurant meant living there. After school, we would sometimes take naps in the back-dining room we reserved for overflow from the main dining room. Hopefully the waiters wouldn't seat anyone back there. But occasionally someone would want to sit in the back-dining room and I would have to pretend to sleep through people's meals. As I lay there, I would consider: what would be more awkward for customers, me suddenly sitting up from a nap or them seeing a sleeping Asian kid in the corner? I would choose the quietest solution.

My father and mother would take their afternoon naps in that back-dining room as well. When they did, my brother and I ran the restaurant. We would take care not to disturb them and to let them rest.

My brother would be in front taking the orders and I would cook. We would switch off. I'm not sure if waiting tables was better or worse. The afternoon shifts were pretty easy. Usually people just wanted a cup of coffee, a burger, or a sandwich. We could handle those. Sometimes they wanted breakfast food. That was easy to prep as well. Now, if they wanted something off the *dinner menu*, we just told them that we ran out of what they wanted.

Every day by the time my father got home, we were already asleep. Every morning when we woke up, we would see him ready to leave for work.

I didn't resent the restaurant or working. I just resented not being like my classmates in private school who went water skiing with their parents – on their own boat; my classmates whose parents came to pick them up in Mercedes. We could never catch up.

~~~

At one point when they sold the restaurant, my father and mother seemed upbeat. They went into real estate. Now our home was filled with boxes of envelopes ready for us to stuff. They bought a car. Actually a new car this time. It was an American car and I remember looking at the green digital speedometer. The car was soft and smelled clean. We rode in it once and my father was proud.

But something went wrong with the sale and the new owners defaulted. Our new car was returned and in its place were a used red Pinto and a blue Oldsmobile. My father was a cook again.

~~~

I focus this essay on those at the lower end of our economically unequal society because their condition and situations are more pronounced. Although there are distress issues relevant for rich and poor, the recession affected middle- and lower-income family's ability to survive and social mobility while among the top earners, the recession affected their intergenerational transmission of wealth and status.

There are two economic worlds.

I'm a psychologist and so I am trying to better understand how people are faring in this system. The problem for all of us is that having money and not having money, and the ways people perceive fairness, creates the same outcome – selfishness, decreased willingness to help others, and interpersonal distance from each other.

For many men, the breadwinner role is inherently full of conflicts. When men attempt to live up to the expectations of being an ideal breadwinner, they run the risk of being consumed by their work. As a consequence, they must either abdicate the role of being a father and caregiver or constantly be in conflict over the right "balance." If the men choose to avoid their role of being a breadwinner, then they run the risk of being labeled lazy, a slacker, and of course, being gay.

Money-on-the-mind is a struggle for many men which sometimes leave them little room for negotiating other ways to be the breadwinning man. There are a great many men who live in that muddled middle of masculine roles and expectations who struggle to cope and contend with situations outside their control. They work hard and do the best they can with what they have.

~~~

The coffee shop opened for breakfast which meant that we had to be in there by 6am. On the weekends, my two brothers and I would go in with my father and open the restaurant. We would unlock the front doors and my father would lock it behind us. We would take our seats at the counter and swing back and forth as fast as we could on the stools. I think that's what caused many of them to eventually wobble and break. My father would go into the kitchen and come out with breakfast for us. Scrambled eggs and diced ham, wheat toast, and a glass of milk for us all – one of three glasses he was sure to make us drink every day. He ate and watched us as we ate. That was enough for him. Once done, we cleared the dishes and replaced the silverware settings we just used. "Always keep your space clean and neat and be courteous to others," good Asian values.

On some weekend afternoons, my mother would take over the restaurant and he would take us to the park to feed the ducks. We used the bread we didn't sell. We always had a lot of bread for the ducks. Other times we would end up at the beach. I don't often remember my parents together with us at the beach; just one at a time.

On some evenings my father would take us to the movies. We never checked the times or what was playing. We just showed up, bought a ticket, watched the last half and then waited for the movie to start again. My brothers and I would sit in front and my father would sit in back. I think he slept.

~~~

I don't speak to my father much. He sometimes calls. I sometimes call. Our conversations are short and stilted.

"How are you?"

"How are you feeling – How is your health?"

"Thank you for the gifts."

He translates what I say into Chinese.

I never ask the question. I save his face and I save mine.

He responds.

"I'm fine."

"How is your family?"

"How is work?"

For a call from Taiwan, our conversation is formal.

"Kut-chee" is what my wife calls it.

When I hang up, my wife looks at me and says "that's it?"

I say, "that's enough for me."

~~~

Once, I came home for a long weekend. I was at home with just my mom. At that time my brother David had been shipped to the Persian Gulf. Part of a light infantry Marine expeditionary force. Desert Storm One. They all joined thinking they would save money for college and now they were headed to war.

I noticed that my mom seemed sad and pensive. She looked like she had been crying for several days. I just assumed it was because of my brother's deployment. I looked at the floor and wall a lot. I didn't know how to take care of my mom. The apartment was not where I had wanted to be, but I needed to be home to get ready for my move to Maryland. I was going to graduate school, finally. It was across the country and I was looking forward to starting a new life.

I was coming out of the bedroom when my mother finally said , "He's gone . . . your father is gone . . . I don't know where he is . . . his things are gone." I walked into my parent's bedroom and into the closets. What would I be looking for? I didn't even know what his things looked like. I only remember him in his work clothes. I saw three or four suit jackets hanging. That was it.

~~~

My father had been affected by poverty his whole life. He just didn't know it and neither did I. He exemplified what the research says about the long-term effects of poverty. It is the lifetime drag, a gravitational pull that constantly works against an individual. The myths of meritocracy and the Protestant Work Ethic only focus on how to achieve without recognizing the baggage and weight many poor and working-class individuals must carry.

What do you think?

1   In this essay, what examples of *affect* do you see that relate to social class? Use specific textual evidence. List any emotions named by the author, as well as any you might infer from the text.
2   What examples of class-relevant *cognition* do you see? Use specific textual evidence. Make sure to notice any shifts in the author's thinking about social class.
3   Using specific textual evidence, indicate where the author mentions specific *behaviors* that are related to matters of social class? What experiences prompted those behaviors?

Psychology and social class: neglectful past but exciting present

As you'll recall, Chapter 1 focused on the complexity inherent in this "thing" called social class. We began the current chapter with the relatively straightforward definition of psychology as the scientific study of behavior and mental process (affect and cognition), and we trust that you were able to find examples of each of these in "The Breadwinner." However, the very nature of psychology forces us back into a position of complexity because psychology is a breathtakingly broad discipline. Many subdisciplines exist, and there are various types of psychology and psychologists. Some branches of the field include clinical and counseling psychology, biological/physiological, cognitive, evolutionary, developmental, social, personality, experimental, learning and behavior, and health psychology. Indeed, if you are majoring or minoring in psychology, you have likely taken courses with these words included in their titles. As additional evidence of our complexity as a field, consider the existence of two major professional organizations: the American Psychological Association (APA) and the Association for Psychological Science (APS). APA breaks itself down into 54 divisions or interest groups, and APS organizes its focus via 60 research topics listed on its website (American Psychological Association, 2021; Association for Psychological Science, 2021).

It should not surprise you, then, that a *psychology of social class* does not lend itself to easy categorization and organization. We might be able to cling for a while to the psychology of social class involving affect, cognition, and behavior related to social class, yet trying to force all the theoretical, research, and practice-oriented work into those three definitional containers would be difficult for us and, frankly, rather boring for you the reader. And while providing an exhaustive history of the ways that psychology has engaged with the topic of social class might be a valuable exercise, our end product would be a different book altogether. Therefore, our purpose with this chapter is not to provide a comprehensive review of how social class has been conceptualized, measured, and researched in psychology. Rather, our intent is to share some important topics, developments, and documents that have emerged over the past couple of decades and to provide you with a sample of some of the more interesting contemporary areas of focus. In some ways, you can think of this chapter as an abbreviated tour of an art museum for people with limited time. Museum brochures typically provide maps that lay out the entire museum for visitors, but sometimes they also provide shortcuts (*If you have just one hour, make sure to see. . . .*) In that spirit, this chapter will offer several "views" of the many rooms of this metaphorical museum and will then provide a brief introduction to the main focus of this book: Will's SCWM-R.

A brief (and select) historical view

If we reach back to the early days of psychology as a discipline (late 1800s and 1900s), we can see that psychologists did not pay much attention to matters of social class or other characteristics deemed to be outside of the *mind*. That's not to say that early social scientists didn't participate in discussions about social class, race, or gender because they most certainly did. For instance, in the late 1800s, Thorstein Veblen identified a phenomenon that he labeled *conspicuous consumption* to describe the ways that the rich exhibited their wealth. But often, theorists and experimentalists asserted that the purest mental states or the best types of minds were those unburdened from matters such as social class, gender, or race. Instead, these matters were seen as troubling issues that plagued the minds of people deemed to be inferior, such as women and African Americans. If you've ever heard people being accused of "playing the race card" or "playing the gender card," perhaps some of that stance sounds familiar.

If we fast-forward 100 years to the end of the last century, anything written about the psychology of social class typically began with assertions about how understudied and neglected this topic was. It is certainly true that contemporary psychology had lagged behind some of the academic disciplines mentioned in previous chapters, most notably sociology. It is also true that psychologists have paid more attention to other social identities/social constructs such as race and sexual orientation than they have to social class. That said, the past couple of decades have seen a substantial uptick in attention to social class. While much of that focus has come from certain subdisciplines (namely, counseling psychology, social psychology, and health psychology), it can now be said that social class research, theory, and practice are being conducted in many corners of the field. Because of these developments, the years 2020 and 2021 presented an exciting and advantageous time for us to be writing this book.

In Table 2.1, we list some important developments in the field, as well as influential documents, such as task force reports and summaries of existing literature. To be clear, this

Table 2.1: Two Decades of Social Class-Related American Psychological Association (APA) Initiatives and Special Issues/Sections of Psychology Journals

Year	Initiative
2000	APA Resolution on Poverty and Socioeconomic Status (SES) (APA, 2000)
2005	APA Task Force on Socioeconomic Status
2007	APA Task Force on SES report on state of social class within psychology (APA, 2007)
2009	APA Task Force report on Psychology's Contribution to End Homelessness
2014	APA Office on Socioeconomic Status's Examining the Complexities Between Health Disparities and Poverty (APA, 2014)
2015	APA's Stop Skipping Class campaign, aimed at helping researchers examine social class and its intersectionality with other social categories (e.g., race, gender)
2017	APA's Multicultural Guidelines… Ecological Approach to Context, Identity, and Intersectionality (of social class, race, gender, etc.) (APA, 2017)
2017	Special Issue, Inequality and Social Class, *Current Opinion in Psychology* (Markus & Stephens, 2017)
2018	Special Issue, Psychological Perspectives on Understanding Socioeconomic Status and Social Class, *Translational Issues in Psychological Science* (Bullock et al., 2018)
2019	Special section of *American Psychologist* focusing on Alleviating Poverty and Economic Inequality (Bullock, 2019)
2019	APA's Guidelines for Psychological Practice for People with Low-Income and Economic Marginalization (APA, 2019)
2019	APA President Rosie Phillips Davis' Deep Poverty Initiative
2019	Special Section: Children's and Adolescents' Understanding and Experiences of Economic Inequality: Implications for Theory, Research, Policy, and Practice, *Developmental Psychology* (Ruck et al., 2019)

list is not an exhaustive compilation of important work in the field. Rather, it represents our combined impression of developments and documents that have changed our thinking about this psychological phenomenon of internalizing the structural.

Making a list and checking it (more than) twice

In 2004, Will and several colleagues (Liu et al., 2004) published a paper in which they asserted that, despite the importance of social class in people's lives, social class had been poorly conceptualized and measured in counseling psychology research. In this review of the published literature in three counseling psychology journals in the 1980s and 1990s, they discovered 448 different terms that had been used to refer to social class, social status, or economic inequality. In their view, researchers were often trying to capture a specific type of social class that they believed impacted an important outcome. Examples include examining how reduced or free school lunch[1] might influence school persistence or trying to understand the enormous variation in how people identify in terms of social class (e.g., the middle–upper working class).

We're going to ask you here to make another kind of list, and we promise it won't have more than 400 items. We'll do this in three steps. First, take a longer look at Table 2.1 and make a list of the specific topics that appear in the documents mentioned (e.g., poverty). You should end up with several different topics. Second, let's examine two examples of scholarship that urge us to reflect upon "where we've been" in the field with regard to social class and where we should go next. The first is Kraus and Stephens's (2012) "roadmap" article, in which they delineate several ways that psychologists can examine social class: as the objective and subjective indicators (discussed briefly in Chapter 1); as an important aspect of context; as a meaningful contributor to our sense of self; as something relevant to our interpersonal interactions; as related to (but distinct from) other measures of rank, power, and status within groups; and as a construct related to race/ethnicity, gender, sexual orientation, and more. If any of these topics are already on your list, ignore them and simply add any topics not already there.

The second article is a more recent "Minding the Gap" article written by Ryan and colleagues (2018). Just the subtitle of the article ("Social Psychological Insights for Strengthening Interclass Relations and Advancing Economic Justice") provides two additional topics for your list: interclass relations and economic justice. In their piece, Ryan et al. hold up three promising areas of focus, which can also be added to your list: how economic scarcity impacts decision-making, the consequences of class privilege, and beliefs about economic mobility and what they call "class permeability."

At this point, you probably have 15 or so items on your list. For a final step, let us add several examples of contemporary social class research that may suggest additional topics to you. For example, if you've ever heard the phrase "retail therapy," you may be interested in research examining whether well–being and sense of self are more influenced by purchasing things vs. purchasing experiences (Carter & Gilovich, 2012; Kumar et al., 2020), Dittmar and colleagues' research on materialism (2014), as well as more recent research conducted by Rice and colleagues (2020) on spending as affective (i.e., emotional) coping.

---

1   It turns out that the topic of school lunch is fertile ground for stories about social class. In the two creative nonfiction essays linked to Chapter 5, both authors (Meliza Bañales and Terri Griffith) discuss their experiences, and we invite your stories at the end of that chapter.

To this list we would add research conducted by Destin and colleagues (e.g., Destin et al., 2017) on status-based identity and economic opportunity and research by Piff and colleagues on links between social class and several constructs of interest to psychology such as happiness (Piff & Moskowitz, 2018), prosocial behavior (Piff & Robinson, 2017), and moral judgment (Côté et al., 2013).

From a more problem-based perspective, there is interesting work being conducted on social exclusion (Smith, 2013), economic inequality and racial economic inequality (Kraus et al., 2019), economic privilege and sense of entitlement (Côté et al., 2020), class-based stereotypes (Durante & Fiske, 2017), and class-based stereotype threat (John-Henderson et al., 2014; Spencer & Castano, 2007). We will discuss classism in Chapters 5 and 6, but here we would also mention recent research in scale development that allows researchers to measure various forms of classism (e.g., Cavalhieri & Chwalisz, 2020; Colbow et al., 2016). Finally, a less-expected intriguing new avenue is an emerging neuroscience of social class. As reviewed by Varnum and Kitayama (2017), particularly promising new areas of research focus on how social class might influence people's attunement to others, their overall cognitive styles (broad vs. narrow), and their perception and evaluation of threat.

If you've done your work here, we suspect you now have a list of roughly 30 topics that are related in some way to social class or are in some way an aspect of what social class is. We encourage you to engage more deeply with this list. (One of Anne's former colleagues used to invite her to "intellectual playdate" lunches, so in a sense, we are inviting you to an intellectual playdate.) One way to approach the list is simply to arrange the various items into clusters of similar items. You might also try to sort items on your list into those definitional categories of affect, behavior, and cognition. Alternatively, you might try and sort them into some of those subdisciplines we mentioned previously: social psychology, cognitive psychology, developmental psychology, etc. Considering that we're concerned in this book with the individual and the structural aspects of social class and classisms, you might also try your hand at arranging items from the most individual (e.g., sense of self, well-being) to the more structural (e.g., poverty, unemployment, inequality, policy).

Whatever form your final list of topics takes, we would argue that it provides a valuable glimpse of what it means to internalize the structural and external aspects of social class. And while the list will not be perfect, it certainly begins to address the question of what a *psychology* of social class *looks like*. If nothing else, this list will certainly substantiate the contention that social class is one of the most meaningful cultural dimensions in people's lives (Liu et al., 2004). A "Discussion Question/Assignment Prompt" at the end of this chapter suggests an additional way to engage with the list.

Theory as container

By now, we've convinced you that the psychology of social class is highly complicated. There are, of course, different approaches we take when faced with intellectual complexity of any kind. We might simply ignore the matter altogether (rarely a good idea), or we might simply choose to simplify matters and focus on one or two aspects of a problem or topic. Most scholars learn early on that "parsimony" is important when designing research. We may want to "study everything" and ask research participants 1,000 questions, but we can't. Therefore we make decisions and take legitimate shortcuts. Another approach is to embrace the complexity and develop a theoretical model that – while maybe not fully comprehensive – strives to be fairly inclusive. A typical definition of a theory is that it is an organized collection of testable ideas, and there is much ongoing discussion in this field (and others) about the nature and importance of theories (e.g., Eronen & Romeijn, 2020). Our point here is that "playing" with your list of topics as we suggest might be a crude simulation of what theory-building actually looks and feels like. Indeed, in being an organized collection of testable ideas, theory serves as a valuable container for the many facets of a problem or topic.

This all brings us to the SCWM-R. Before we introduce the model and present the remaining chapters of this textbook, we wish to make three important points. First, the SCWM-R is not the only psychological theory concerned with social class. Second, we don't claim that the model is perfect or fully comprehensive. Sometimes people talk about theory as a "heuristic device" – a jumping-off point for further exploration, and we urge you to consider the SCWM-R in that light. Third, the original theory (the SCWM) and its revision (the SCWM-R) were launched, respectively, in 2004 and 2011. Therefore, we are not claiming that the theory was developed as a way to deal with all possible social class–related topics. Rather, it was developed to provide an antidote to the mostly *objective* constructions of social class that used various indices of social class (e.g., income, education) to construct numerous – and sometimes almost meaningless – different social class groupings, while treating classism as something adjacent to social class rather than something quite integral.

One approach to the complexity: the SCWM-R

Figure 2.1 provides a basic diagram of the SCWM-R.

As Figure 2.1 indicates, the SCWM-R contains multiple components, and the rest of this textbook will provide a deep focus on each component and the many interconnections

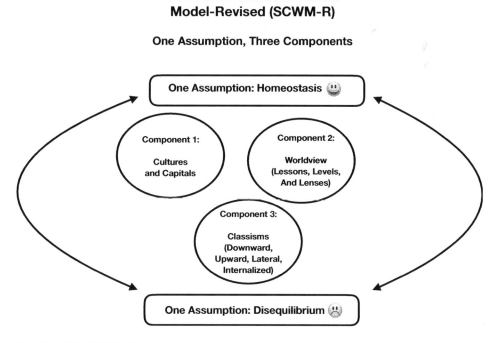

Figure 2.1: The SCWM-R

among them. But for now, we offer a helpful shortcut or tagline as an introduction to the model: One Assumption, Three Components.

One assumption

As stated previously when we "stood" on the metaphorical ladder,[2] there is value in considering how we see ourselves in relation to others on the ladder and how we interact with similar or dissimilar others. If you've ever stood on an actual ladder, keeping your balance was probably a central consideration. The major assumption of the SCWM-R (shown in the rectangles with large arrows running through them) is that people are motivated toward a sense of constancy, balance, and equilibrium with regard to social class, a state that the model calls *Homeostasis*. In other words, we all strive toward a general feeling of "okayness," "normalness," and in some ways "averageness" in terms of our social class standing. Conversely, the SCWM-R claims that people are motivated to avoid feeling "not okay" about their social class standing, a state known as *Disequilibrium*.

Think about the last time you were in a situation in which you felt out of place in terms of your social class. More specifically, can you think about a time when you felt surrounded by people of a higher or lower social class than you? The SCWM-R suggests that situations such as these might put us, even if just temporarily, into a state of Disequilibrium, of feeling less okay about who we are as social class beings. For example, we might overhear a comment that we deem to be classist. Or we might feel under-dressed, or self-conscious, or even "lesser than." Because these feelings are uncomfortable, we are motivated to return ourselves to Homeostasis, to feeling generally okay with who we are as social class beings. And, as will be discussed in later chapters, we adopt certain attitudes or enact certain behaviors in order to get ourselves there. Further, because many of us engage in various contexts that put us in touch with people from a variety of social class positions, we may shift back and forth between these two states of Homeostasis and Disequilibrium on a fairly regular basis.[3]

Component 1: cultures and capitals

Most of us spend time on any given day, week, or month in a variety of contexts. For example, one might spend time at home with immediate family members, go to a workplace, attend school, have visits with extended family members, regularly visit a house of worship, spend time in government agencies or community-based organizations, hang out with friends, engage in neighborhood or community events, interact with the medical establishment, work out at a gym, engage with professional organizations . . . the list could go on and on.

The SCWM-R encourages us to consider these contexts as *Economic Cultures* (ECs). ECs play various roles. They help us make sense of how social class operates and situates us within local and larger aspects of our world. They make certain demands of us with regard to social class (known in the model as forms of *Capital*). And they determine what we need to do to maintain our social class standing or our place on the ladder. In these

---

2 We'll discuss the ladder metaphor more fully in Chapter 3 and compare it with a metaphorical scaffold.
3 Here and in the next three chapters, we will capitalize terms that represent pieces of the SCWM-R. We do this to differentiate the terms as specifically used in the model from more general uses of the term.

ways, ECs conduct the important work of helping us develop and refine our Social Class Worldviews. ECs and the forms of Capital they demand will be defined more formally and described in more detail in the next chapter, Chapter 3.

Component 2: worldview: lessons, levels, and lenses

The second component of the SCWM-R describes how individuals come to see social class operating in the world and begin to understand the world through the lens of social class (the Worldview). One way that Worldviews develop is through Socialization Messages, implicit or explicit, from parents, other family members, peers, and institutions. Worldviews also develop via ever-evolving levels of Consciousness about Social Class and Classism. We may begin, for example, with little or no awareness about social class and classism, and we may end up with an ever-evolving, highly complex, and sophisticated understanding of these factors. A final important aspect of our Worldview involves the specific lenses we use to see class in the world: the lens of material possessions, the lens of class-related behaviors, and the lens of lifestyle. Development of the Worldview will be described more fully in Chapter 4.

Component 3: forms of classism

In the psychological literature, classism is typically defined as looking down upon someone who is poor (Colbow et al., 2016). The SCWM-R treats classism in a much broader way, with four forms specified and referred to as *classisms*: Downward Classism, Upward Classism, Lateral Classism, and Internalized Classism. An important contribution of the SCWM-R is that we *experience* classisms but also *enact* classisms, for example, as a way to restore the Homeostasis mentioned previously. Classisms are also integral in how we understand the formation and maintenance of the various social classes, and we will say more about classisms in Chapter 5.

But what about race . . . and gender . . . and . . . ?

This book focuses on the revised version of the SCWM, which made two important contributions: focusing on people's shifting levels of awareness and consciousness of social class and emphasizing that we cannot examine social class without also examining classism (Liu, 2011a, 2011b). In other words, we can't see social class as a form of identity or as a way of seeing the world without also looking at how social class is organized by society – by forces outside of and larger than our individual selves. Talking about social class merely as identity can give the mistaken impression that social class is all about, and only about, individual selves.

But *how we identify* is caught up with *how others identify us*. The ECs that we'll discuss in the next chapter also direct us to see that social class and classisms serve an important function in society that is inflected in how we see ourselves and how others see us. And we know that cultures assign meaning and value to these various identities and identifications. This idea of meaning-making points to social class as a social construction or a social construct. And as Settles and colleagues (2020) put it "interrelated power structures inform subjective experiences of social identities, such that a person's social group membership (e.g., race) cannot be understood without also understanding the other social groups to which they belong (e.g., gender and class)." Thus, the idea of social class as identity and worldview has to be understood vis-à-vis the institutions that create and maintain inequality, and we have to attend to power dynamics, access to resources, and matters of inequity. Returning to that basic definition of psychology, understanding the ways that people think, act, and feel with regard to social class should only be the beginning of our understanding.

Of course, social class is not the only characteristic involving self-identification, identification of and by others, social group membership, and the assignment of meaning. There are various other characteristics to which we assign meaning – for example, someone's race, gender, sexual orientation, gender identity, religious/spiritual beliefs and practices, immigration status, or disability/ability status. And, it must also be said that there are multiple forms of oppression to which we humans subject one another, based upon these and other characteristics. Assigning power, resources, and value to one group over another might seem silly, random, and arbitrary, such as the decision to sort people into meaningful groups on the basis of foot size or length of hair. Yet when we add ideas about power, access to resources, different levels of valuing, and inequity, we begin to see that such matters are not random and are far more serious.

Therefore, in a similar way to not being able to discuss social class without also talking about multiple forms of classism (classisms), it is difficult to talk about one form of oppression – such as classism – without simultaneously considering other forms, such as racism. Leonardo (2012) refers to "the coordinated but awkward dance between race and class" (p. 429) and offers the singular word *raceclass* to declare that we can't really talk about social class without also examining how we think about race and racism.

The simultaneous consideration of multiple forms of oppression is not a new phenomenon, either in the discipline of psychology or in the wider world of scholarship (Cole, 2009; Collins, 2000; Crenshaw, 1989; Settles et al., 2020). The term *intersectionality* has come into prominence as the term of use for this simultaneous consideration (Collins & Bilge, 2020), and it has become a somewhat controversial idea in the polarized "culture wars" of the past few decades. More important, scholars focusing on intersectionality have issued criticism as well: that we too quickly forget its roots in Black feminist thought (Buchanan & Wiklund, 2021; Collins, 2000; Lewis et al., 2017; Moradi et al., 2020), that we limit ourselves to conceptualizing intersectionality as only being about identity (Shin et al., 2017), or that we tend to avoid the social justice-oriented meaning and history of the term (Buchanan & Wiklund, 2021).

Shin and colleagues (2017) have provided a useful framework for evaluating these critiques. In their content analysis of intersectionality scholarship published in two major counseling psychology journals, they extend existing models differentiating between weak (identity only) and strong approaches to intersectionality by proposing a third – *transformative* – approach, one that focuses on "multiple social identities and structural inequality *and* explicitly calls for social justice action aimed at dismantling systems of oppression" (p. 460).

So, what is *our approach* to intersectionality, and how will we engage with the concept? After all, this book has social class in the title but no other social identity/social construct. Looking back at Figure 2.1, where do these other social identities/social constructs (such as race) belong in the SCWM-R? As people who write and teach about social class, we know that doing so often means striking a delicate balance. On the one hand, we argue that holding social class up to the light – by itself and in *temporary* isolation from other factors – is valuable and necessary, and you'll see that we do that a fair amount in this book. But we also know that this approach is not enough. Thus, throughout this book,

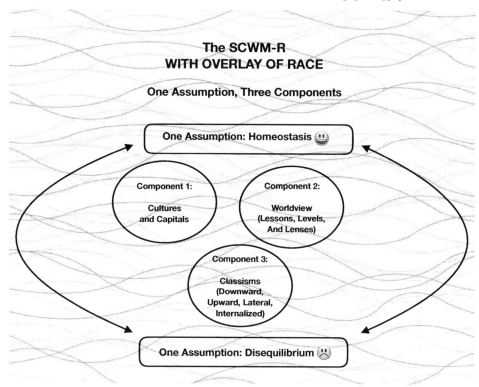

Figure 2.2: The SCWM-R, with overlay of race and racism

as we discuss and describe social class and classisms, we address how race and racism are also particularly relevant. Figure 2.2 depicts one possible way to visualize race (and racism) and social class (and classisms) together. In this illustration, race and racism can be seen as a transparent overlay to the SCWM-R. All the components of the model still exist, but all components, and their various interrelations, are now seen through the overlay of race and racism. Just as the wavy lines run through the diagram, we can see race and racism "running through" the lived experience of social class and classism.

We admit that, historically, scholars and activists have sometimes urged the simultaneous consideration of more than two social constructs. Consider, for example, the Combahee River Collective's 1977 statement against "racial, sexual, heterosexual, and class oppression" (p. 1); Collins (2015) pointing to the "placeholder umbrella term" of race, class, and gender; and the offering of courses named "Race, Class, and Gender" at many colleges and universities. As people who have written and taught about gender and sexual orientation, we will say we're not completely comfortable paying relatively scant attention to these constructs. However, as the writer George Saunders (Saunders, 2021) points out, all writing (and rewriting) involves thousands of small decisions, and one decision we made as authors was that this book would focus primarily on the intersection of social class and race.

More specifically, the next three chapters of the book will focus on the components of the SCWM-R, and in those chapters, we will argue that it's critically important to consider how BIPOC experience social class and classism differently than do White people. In some places, we will make that point, and in some places, we'll ask you to consider this more fully in a ***Discussion Question***. Thus, at the end of each of the following chapters, we provide an Intersectionality Check-In that asks you to consider how the model components being discussed might be experienced differently by different populations. And where you feel moved to consider how social class intersects with a social identity/social construct that is more salient to you and your story (e.g., gender, sexual orientation), we hope that you will engage in that way. This is, after all, a book committed to the power of stories, and your story matters. In our final chapter, Chapter 6, Will revisits and recenters race and racism within his model of class and classism.

Let us make two final points here. First, as we mentioned previously, 2020 and 2021 proved to be an advantageous time to write this book given the richness of contemporary scholarship on social class and classism, and this is also true about writing, as psychologists, about intersectionality. As Grzanka and colleagues (2020) say, intersectionality has moved "from the margins to the mainstream," and McCormick-Huhn and colleagues (2019) ask, "What if psychologists took intersectionality seriously?" We intend to do so in this book, as we endeavor to do in all of our other work as psychologists.

Second, as we mentioned earlier the concept of intersectionality has attracted some controversy. It has been criticized widely, frequently by people unaware of its roots in actual rigorous scholarship, and has become part of the polarized culture wars that have informed American politics and conversation for the past few decades. Our intent here is not to wade into culture-war conversations about specific areas of scholarship other than to remark that similar criticism has been leveled at other forms of scholarship pioneered by scholars of Color (e.g., racial microaggressions and, more recently, the entire field of Critical Race Theory).

Rather, as psychologists, we will use this space to affirm our commitment – individually and collectively – to seek to understand human experience in all its vastness and diversity. Or, to use the words of Collins and Bilge (2020), we seek "more expansive understandings of individual and collective identities" (p. 114). We consider doing so to be an ethical, moral, and professional obligation, and we know that our own positionalities figure in here as well. As an Asian person and a White person, we are aware that we experience social class and race differently from one another, and differently from others with different positionalities vis-à-vis these social identities/social constructs.

Discussion questions/assignment prompts

1   Knowing what you know from reading this chapter, how would you answer the question "What does a *psychology* of social class look like?"
2   At the beginning of the chapter, we asked you to find examples of social class–related affect, behavior, and cognition in "The Breadwinner." How many examples from your topics list can you find in that essay?
3   Intersectionality Check-In: Will identifies as an Asian American man. In his essay "The Breadwinner," how many specific instances do you see of the intersection of class and race, and class and gender? How might the specifics of his narrative have been different for someone who is White and/or someone who is a woman?
4   Digital Spotlight: Revisit your topics list and identify which topics you tend to see on social media, and which topics are less represented. Which platforms (e.g., Instagram,

TikTok) are more likely, and which are less likely, to feature the topics you identify? As always, share why you think that might be the case.

5 What's Your Story? Which items on your topics less are most personally relevant for you? In other words, which topics most closely align with your lived experience of social class and classism? Discuss a few of the most relevant topics.

References

American Psychological Association. (2007). *Report of the APA task force on socioeconomic status.* www.apa.org/pi/ses/resources/publications/task-force-2006.pdf

American Psychological Association. (2014). *Examining the complexities between health disparities and poverty.* www.apa.org/pi/ses/resources/poverty-complexities-bibliography.pdf

American Psychological Association. (2017). *Multicultural guidelines: An ecological approach to context, identity, and intersectionality.* www.apa.org/about/policy/multicultural-guidelines.pdf

American Psychological Association. (2019). *Guidelines for psychological practice for people with low income and economic marginalization.* www.apa.org/about/policy/guidelines-low-income.pdf

American Psychological Association. (2021, May 18). *Divisions of APA.* www.apa.org/about/division

Association for Psychological Science. (2021, May 18). *Research topics.* www.psychologicalscience.org/topics/research-topics

Buchanan, N.T., & Wiklund, L.O. (2021). Intersectionality research in psychological science: Resisting the tendency to disconnect, dilute, and depoliticize. *Research on Child and Adolescent Psychopathology, 49,* 25–31.

Bullock, H.E. (2019). Psychology's contributions to understanding and alleviating poverty and economic inequality: Introduction to the special section. *American Psychologist, 74*(6), 635–640. http://dx.doi.org/10.1037/amp0000532

Bullock, H.E., Griffin, K.M., Kent, A.H., & Toolis, E.E. (2018). Editorial: Translating psychological research on social class and socioeconomic status. *Translational Issues in Psychology, 4*(2), 119–121. http://dx.doi.org/10.1037/tps0000160

Carter, T.J., & Gilovich, T. (2012). I am what I do, not what I have: The differential centrality of experiential and material purchases to the self. *Journal of Personality and Social Psychology, 102*(6), 1304–1317. https://doi.org/10.1037/a0027407; https://doi.org/10.1177/0011000019899395

Cavalhieri, K.E., & Chwalisz, K. (2020). Development and initial validation of the perceived experiences of classism scale. *The Counseling Psychologist, 48*(3), 310–341. https://doi.org/10.1177/0011000019899395

Colbow, A.J., Cannella, E., Vispoel, W., Morris, C.A., Cederberg, C., Conrad, M., Rice, A.J., & Liu, W.M. (2016). Development of the classism attitudinal profile (CAP). *Journal of Counseling Psychology, 63*(5), 571–585. http://dx.doi.org/10.1037/cou0000169

Cole, E.R. (2009). Intersectionality and research in psychology. *American Psychologist, 64*(3), 170–180. https://doi.org/10.1037/a0014564

Collins, P.H. (2000). *Black feminist thought.* New York, NY: Routledge.

Collins, P.H. (2015). Intersectionality's definition dilemmas. *Annual Review of Sociology, 41,* 1–20.

Collins, P.H., & Bilge, S. (2020). *Intersectionality* (2nd ed.). New York, NY: Wiley.

Combahee River Collective. (1977). *The Combahee river collective statement.* www.blackpast.org/african-american-history/combahee-river-collective-statement-1977/

Côté, S., Piff, P.K., & Willer, R. (2013). For whom do the ends justify the means? Social class and utilitarian moral judgment. *Journal of Personality and Social Psychology, 104*(3), 490–503. https://doi.org/10.1037/a0030931

Côté, S., Stellar, J.E., Willer, R., Forbes, R.C., Martin, S.R., & Bianchi, E. (2020). The psychology of entrenched privilege: High socioeconomic status individuals from affluent backgrounds are uniquely high in entitlement. *Personality and Social Psychology Bulletin, 47*(1), 70–88. https://doi.org/10.1177/0146167220916633

Crenshaw, K. (1989.) Demarginalizing the intersection of race and sex: A Black feminist theory and antiracist practice. *University of Chicago Legal Forum, 1*(8), 139–167. http://chicagounbound.uchicago.edu/uclf/vol1989/iss1/8

Destin, M., Rheinschmidt-Same, M., & Richeson, J.A. (2017). Status-based identity: A conceptual approach integrating the social psychological study of socioeconomic status and identity. *Perspectives on Psychological Science, 12*(2), 270–289. https://doi.org/10.1177/1745691616664424

Dittmar, H., Bond, R., Hurst, M., & Kasser, T. (2014). The relationship between materialism and well-being: A meta-analysis. *Journal of Personality and Social Psychology, 107*(5), 879–924. http://dx.doi.org/10.1037/a0037409

Durante, F., & Fiske, S.T. (2017). How social class stereotypes maintain inequality. *Current Opinion in Psychology, 18*, 43–48. http://dx.doi.org/10.1016/j.copsyc.2017.07.033

Eronen, M.I., & Romejin, J.W. (2020). Philosophy of science and the formalization of psychological theory. *Theory & Psychology, 30*(6), 786–799. https://doi.org/10.1177%2F0959354320969876

Grzanka, P.R., Flores, M.J., VanDaalen, R.A., & Velez, G. (2020). Intersectionality in psychology: Translational science for social justice. *Translational Issues in Psychological Science, 6*(4), 304–313. https://doi.org/10.1037/tps0000276

John-Henderson, N., Rheinschmidt, M.L., Mendoza-Denton, R., & Francis, D.D. (2014). Performance and inflammation outcomes are predicted by different facets of socioeconomic status under stereotype threat. *Social Psychological and Personality Science, 5*(3), 301–309. https://doi.org/10.1177/1948550613494226

Kraus, M.W., Onyeador, I.N., Daumeyer, N.M., Rucker, J.M., & Richeson, J.A. (2019). The misperception of racial economic inequality. *Perspectives on Psychological Science, 14*(6), 899–921. https://doi.org/10.1177%2F1745691619863049

Kraus, M.W., & Stephens, N. (2012). A roadmap for an emerging psychology of social class. *Social and Personality Psychology Compass, 6*(9), 642–656.https://doi.org/10.1111/j.1751-9004.2012.00453.x

Kumar, A., Killingsworth, M.A., & Gilovich, T. (2020). Spending on doing promotes more moment-to-moment happiness than spending on having. *Journal of Experimental Social Psychology, 88*, 1–6. https://doi.org/10.1016/j.jesp.2020.103971

Leonardo, Z. (2012). The race for class: Reflections on a critical raceclass theory of education. *Educational Studies, 48*(5), 427–449. https://doi.org/10.1080/00131946.2012.715831

Lewis, J.A., Williams, M.G., Peppers, E.J., & Gadson, C.A. (2017). Apply intersectionality to explore the relations between gendered racism and health among Black women. *Journal of Counseling Psychology, 64*(5), 475–486. http://dx.doi.org/10.1037/cou0000231

Liu, W.M. (2011a). *Social class and classism in the helping professions: Research, theory, and practice.* Thousand Oaks, CA: Sage Publications.

Liu, W.M. (2011b). Developing a social class and classism consciousness. In E.M. Altmaier & J.C. Hansen (Eds.), *The Oxford handbook of counseling psychology* (pp. 326–345). New York, NY: Oxford University Press.

Liu, W.M., Ali, S.R., Soleck, G., Hopps, J., Dunston, K., & Pickett, T., Jr. (2004). Using social class in counseling psychology research. *Journal of Counseling Psychology, 51*(1), 3–18. https://doi.org/10.1037/0022-0167.51.1.3

McCormick-Huhn, K., Warner, L.H., Settles, I.H., & Shields, S.A. (2019). What if psychology took intersectionality seriously? Changing how psychologists think about participants. *Psychology of Women Quarterly, 43*(4), 445–456. https://doi.org/10.1177/0361684319866430

Moradi, B., Parent, M.C., Weis, A.S., Ouch, S., & Broad, K.L. (2020). Mapping the travels of intersectionality scholarship: A citation network analysis. *Psychology of Women Quarterly, 44*(2), 151–169. https://doi.org/10.1177/0361684320902408

Piff, P.K., & Moskowitz, J.P. (2018). Wealth, poverty, and happiness: Social class is differentially associated with positive emotions. *Emotion, 18*(6), 902–905. http://dx.doi.org/10.1037/emo0000387

Piff, P.K., & Robinson, A.R. (2017). Social class and prosocial behavior: Current evidence, caveats, and questions. *Current Opinion in Psychology, 18*, 6–10. https://doi.org/10.1016/j.copsyc.2017.06.003

Rice, A., Garrison, Y.L., & Liu, W.M. (2020). Spending as social and affective coping (SSAC): Measure development and initial validation. *The Counseling Psychologist*, 48(1), 78–105. https://doi.org/10.177/001100019878848

Ruck, M.D., Mistry, R.S., & Flanagan, C.A. (2019). Children's and adolescents' understanding and experiences of economic inequality: An introduction to the special section. *Developmental Psychology*, 55(3), 449–456. http://dx.doi.org/10.1037/dev0000694

Ryan, D.A., Singh, M.R., Hentschke, E.A., & Bullock, H.E. (2018). "Minding the gap": Social psychological insights for strengthening interclass relations and advancing economic justice. *Translational Issues in Psychological Science*, 4(2), 187–197. https://doi.org/10.1037/tps0000158

Saunders, G. (2021). *A swim in a pond in the rain*. New York: Random House.

Settles, I.H., Warner, L.R., Buchanan, N.T. and Jones, M.K. (2020). Understanding psychology's resistance to intersectionality theory using a framework of epistemic exclusion and invisibility. *Journal of Social Issues*, 76: 796–813. https://doi.org/10.1111/josi.12403

Shin, R.Q., Welch, J.C., Kaya, A.E., Yeung, J.G., Obama, C., Sharma, R., Vernay, C.N., & Yee, S. (2017). The intersectionality framework and identity intersections in *Counseling Psychology* and *The Counseling Psychologist*: A content analysis. *Journal of Counseling Psychology*, 64(5), 458–474. http://dx.doi.org/10.1037/cou0000204

Smith, L. (2013). So close and yet so far away: Social class, social exclusion, and mental health practice. *American Journal of Orthopsychiatry*, 83(1), 11–16. https://doi.org/10.1111/ajop.12008

Spencer, B., & Castano, E. (2007). Social class is dead. Long live social class! Stereotype threat among low socioeconomic status individuals. *Social Justice Research*, 20, 418–432. https://doi.org/10.1007/s11211-007-0047-7

Varnum, M.E.W., & Kitayama, S. (2017). The neuroscience of social class. *Current Opinion in Psychology*, 18, 147–151. https://doi.org/10.1016/j.copsyc.2017.07.032

3   Economic cultures and capital demands

Component 1 of the SCWM-R

Accompanying Essay(s): J.D. Scrimgeour, "A Good School";
Tina Fakhrid-Deen, "Ghetto Fabulous"

Check your comprehension

- The SCWM-R is chiefly concerned with the way individuals make subjective, internal, or intrapsychic meaning out of the more objective, external, or structural aspects of social class.
- Multiple definitions of social class exist, ranging from quite simple ones to more complicated versions that include phenomena such as beliefs and perceptions, boundaries, sense of belonging, status ordering, and culture. Many of those previous definitions reflect attempts by researchers to make sense of how people exist within certain social class categories (e.g., lower middle class).
- The major assumption underlying the SCWM-R is that individuals are motivated away from the Disequilibrium that comes from thinking negatively about themselves in a given social class position.
- Conversely, we are motivated toward the Homeostasis (constancy or "okayness") that comes from maintaining or establishing one's standing in a given social class.

What do you think?

- Do you ever have the experience when you move from context to context (say, from home to school to work) that very different behaviors or attitudes are expected of you? How much of that has to do with social class?
- Do you ever feel bad about yourself in terms of social class? Do you ever find that you compare yourself to others? Do you ever sense that people own more possessions than you do or are living a lifestyle that you'd like to have? How do you help to ease that sense of Disequilibrium?
- What specific feelings arise for you (e.g., a tinge of anxiety? Frustration? Resentment?) when you realize you may not have the latest phone, computer, or item of clothing?

What are economic cultures?

Most of us spend time in any given day, week, or month in a variety of contexts. For example, one might

- spend time at home with immediate family members,
- go to a workplace,

DOI: 10.4324/9780429317606-4

- attend school,
- have visits with extended family members,
- attend services at a house of worship,
- spend time in government agencies or community-based organizations,
- hang out with friends,
- engage in neighborhood or community events,
- interact with the medical establishment,
- work out at a gym,
- engage with professional organizations,
- and the list could go on and on.

How and where do you spend your time? Take a minute right now to consider all of the specific contexts in which you spend time on a fairly regular basis. While these contexts may hold various meanings for you (e.g., as sources of great joy or frustration, or both, depending on the day), the SCWM-R encourages us to consider these contexts as *ECs*. ECs are defined in the model as *environments or contexts that (1) help us make sense of how social class operates in the world and (2) determine what resources and characteristics are expected of us to maintain our social class standing*. ECs can be quite local (or can be thought of as *localized ecologies*), but they also are tied to larger systems of how social class (and gender, race, and so on) function in our society. In these ways, ECs conduct the important work of helping us develop and refine our Social Class Worldviews, and worldviews will be discussed more in-depth in the next chapter. For now, our task will be understanding how ECs perform the two functions just mentioned.

Making sense of how social class operates

How does social class actually "work"? A major function of ECs is to help us make sense of how social class operates. Think back to those objective indicators of SES discussed previously (income, wealth, education level, and occupational status) and recall that the SCWM-R cares about how individuals make subjective (or internal or intrapsychic) meaning out of these more objective (or external or structural) aspects. As an example, imagine how income that comes from paid employment would take on one meaning to someone with vast amounts of inherited wealth, compared to someone who lives pay-check to paycheck. The ECs in which those people live, work, and interact have helped them develop these different understandings of income. Imagine also how an unexpected inheritance of $5,000 would likely be understood quite differently by these two people.

Different ECs might also cultivate different beliefs about occupations. Having a 23-year-old offspring working as a barista might be a source of pride for a family with a long and proud tradition in the service industry but less a source of pride in a family full of doctors and lawyers. Similarly, in the ECs of some families, completing a college degree is seen as a tremendous accomplishment, while in others, graduating college might be seen as merely a stepping-stone toward a master's degree or a PhD.

The neighborhoods in which we live can be seen as ECs, and they usually have certain explicit and tangible boundaries such as highways, bridges, and railroad tracks. For example, think about where your neighborhood begins (e.g., east of the river) and where it ends (e.g. downtown). Sometimes, these different ECs can be quite similar and exist adjacent to each other, and so a person familiar with their own EC can easily move into and feel comfortable in another EC. Other times, of course, moving across ECs may represent significant shifts in expectations and resources, and a person moving into an unfamiliar EC may experience tension and distress because of those shifts but perhaps also because of disparities in resources between the ECs. Someone who is a first-generation college student, for example, may feel the usual new intellectual demands of higher education, but they may also experience unique distress due to different expectations about financial resources and expenditures (e.g., clothing, laboratory fees, a new computer).

In some ECs we might find worldviews that are similar to our own, while other ECs may be much more challenging. In Chapter 2, we asked you about a time in which you entered an environment and felt out of place in terms of your social class, perhaps because you felt the pressure of Downward Classism (i.e., people seeing you or treating you in a way that suggested you were in a social class beneath them). Given that we are motivated *toward* social class–based Homeostasis and *away from* the Disequilibrium that Downward Classism and other classisms can cause, it is easy to see why people might stay in economic-cultural contexts that are familiar and more comfortable. Indeed, given the pull of Homeostasis, it's not surprising that some people spend most of their lives in the comfort of these familiar ECs, thereby developing a very narrow sense of EC, in general, and a limited understanding of people who inhabit other EC contexts. Further, because social class and classisms intersect in important ways with race and racism, homogeneous ECs can also be rather racially homogenous, leaving us with little understanding of the racialized economic experiences of people in different racial groups.

Thus far we've discussed ECs that exist at a close-to-the-individual "micro" level, for example, one's family or neighborhood. But ECs also exist at the more "macro" level. Macro-level ECs involve forces that exert their influence on individuals but do so from more of a distance. Take for example a country's overall economic system. One way that the capitalist system of the United States exerts influence on people is by valuing certain resources and characteristics over other resources and characteristics. Because capitalism, which we will later discuss as racialized capitalism, has always focused on individual property ownership and rights, *having things* is a crucial aspect of social class and classism in the United States.

Within a capitalist society, *having things*, especially *having more things*, means that one is closer to being a capitalist (owner and elite) than a worker; recall Marx's demarcation of two classes: the working class and the owning class. Through subtle lessons about what is valued, a macro-level economic system imparts lessons about how class operates, and it pressures people to make sense of class in certain ways. Individuals in the United States may feel pressured to *have things* more than someone from, say, a Democratic Socialist country such as Denmark would. For example, in the United States, homeownership is highly valued in many sectors of society, so individuals in their 30s might feel pressure to purchase property. But countries vary greatly in their rates of homeownership (Andrews & Sánchez, 2011), and this pressure to own is neither universally applied nor experienced. For a member of the working classes, then, *having things* can be a proxy for feeling more empowered and being able to have agency over one's life, much like the wealthy, owning-class capitalist. From this standpoint, property ownership is not simply about one's materialism or materialistic attitudes and proclivity toward consumerism and buying but is ingrained in how we come to see ourselves.

For another example of a macro-level EC, consider celebrity culture in the United States. It's especially interesting to examine how it shows up every day on social media, in advertising, and perhaps in its grandest display: on awards nights. Most people are not able to afford the high-end designer purses, shoes, and jewelry that are conspicuously displayed at these events, much less the extravagant gowns and tuxedos of the red carpet. But this performance of fashion or style (in other words, this *aesthetic*) serves to define the look of wealth, affluence, and fame.

This macro-level aesthetic is then distilled for the wider population at more micro-levels. To the extent that people feel expectations or pressure to reproduce these macro-level looks of celebrity culture, they can purchase similar knockoff fashions at an array of stores marketed for different social class groups. These stores may range from specialty boutiques and larger chain retailers specializing in certain looks (e.g., Anthropologie or Free People or J. Crew) to higher-end department stores such as Lord and Taylor or Neiman Marcus, to chain retailers considered more affordable, ranging from Macy's and Target to Primark or Walmart.

Ironically, as much as we love brands (e.g., Langner & Schmidt, 2015), the EC of the United States also seems to adore people who engage in conspicuous "non-branding" of themselves. Think of some of the White male CEOs of companies like Facebook or Twitter who eschew corporate uniforms (suits and ties) and adopt another uniform of hoodies, jeans, and sneakers. Celebrities also partake in this non-branding, showing up in T-shirts and jeans from specific high-fashion name brands that don't clearly identify the fashion houses from which they come, and this aesthetic is likewise distilled for onlookers and fans.

In addition to considering how macro-level systems help individuals make sense of class-related phenomena (such as whether to pursue homeownership or how much money to spend to be stylish), it's also important to consider how different macro-level systems might exert different influences on micro-level contexts such as one's family, neighborhood, or other institutions. As an example, think about how the relative strength of the U.S. economy (macro-EC) might impact a specific working-class neighborhood (micro-EC). In times of a robust economy, the employment rate in the neighborhood might be high, local businesses might be thriving, and the infrastructure of the neighborhood (e.g., roads, bridges, parks) might be in great shape. In more depressed economic times (e.g., the Great Recession of 2008 or the pandemic economy of 2021), that same neighborhood might experience higher unemployment, small businesses shutting down, or bridges and roads that need repair. Yet those same economic downturns may have less impact on an upper-middle-class neighborhood.

Recall the earlier point that micro-level ECs, in addition to being somewhat homogenous with respect to social class and classism, can be racially homogenous as well. This homogeneity may cause people who inhabit one particular EC to lack sensitivity or familiarity with the stresses and problems of other ECs. It is no surprise, then, when we discover that people from different ECs can hold vastly different perceptions about the problems of economic inequality and inequities (Belle, 2006; Horowitz et al., 2020; Markus & Stephens, 2017). Similarly, members of a predominantly White EC may see an economic downturn strictly as a problem of social class and economics and may have a difficult time understanding how race and racism come into play. Since they don't perceive race as a culture or identity intimately connected to the struggles that an economic depression may cause, those people will have a hard time seeing race and racism as a meaningful intersecting problem with social class and classism. However, people in a more racially diverse community or EC will likely have more insight into this intertwining of social class and race.

Expecting (and demanding?) certain resources and characteristics

We've talked a fair amount at this point about pressures, perhaps subtle, to live out social class in a certain way. The SCWM-R uses the term *capital* to represent the various expectations and demands that ECs, macro and micro, impose on individuals. The term *capital* has a long history in the social sciences, with most theoretical models distinguishing among several forms of capital and some as many as ten.[1] *Capital* is defined in the SCWM-R as *resources or characteristics that are valued by specific ECs and expected of (perhaps demanded of) individuals in order to maintain their social class position.* The SCWM-R depicts three specific forms: *Human Capital, Social Capital,* and *Cultural Capital.*

As we explain each form of capital, please keep in mind that we may not always value these forms of capital equally. Rather, depending on the context, each type of capital may be differently meaningful – or *salient* – for us. In different ECs, or even at different points in our lives, we may focus primarily on developing one form of capital while the others are developed as auxiliary (i.e., backup or reserve) capitals. We'll use an example of a college or university professor. Depending on the professor's academic discipline, career stage, or other aspects of their context, one form of capital (e.g., attaining a certain education level) may be a priority, and the auxiliary capitals may be placed on the proverbial back burner. To extend this example, you may have heard the adage "It's not what you know, it's *who* you know." In this instance, "who you know" can be considered a form of capital, but one that is deemed less important at the moment than another form of capital (e.g., "what you know").

Human capital

In the SCWM-R, Human Capital can be defined as *the capabilities and physical characteristics with which we are born and/or that we develop and enhance through our lives.* For example, each of us is born with a brain that is wired for learning, and intelligence and related ability may be developed and enhanced through formal education or training. In the ECs of the college or university, the "what you know" part of the adage used previously is typically the most important aspect of Human Capital. In other words, education level and being considered "smart" in one's particular field are critically important, especially at the beginning of one's career. In this context, people are highly motivated to present themselves as smart because doing so may determine their social class position and help them achieve upward economic and social mobility – that is, help them climb the socio-economic ladder.

As another example, in the EC of professional athleticism, the valued characteristics might be body size, muscularity, speed, strength, or endurance. These forms of Human Capital are an important part of social class position because athletic performance is typically related to pay and to longer-term contracts. Finally, in contexts in which beauty and physical attractiveness are important, people may feel enormous pressure to obtain or maintain these qualities for the purposes of social class position. Examples here include

---

1   Research on certain "vulnerable populations" (e.g., minoritized individuals, first-generation college students) frequently highlights forms of capital that people lack. However, theorists such as Yosso (2005) have urged us to look beyond such deficiency models and investigate overlooked forms of capital that such groups might possess – e.g., aspirational capital (strong motivation to succeed), linguistic capital (being bilingual or multilingual), or navigational capital (being able to move through spaces not designed with you in mind).

celebrity culture, some corners of the news media, and of course the world of social media influencers.

What we start to understand, even with something that should be objective like learning and education, is that Human Capital demands and expectations are subjective and tied to specific ECs. Education, for example, is valued by some, and for others, the value of education is explicitly linked to one's institutional pedigree (e.g., an Ivy League school name). Having an Ivy League degree does not make one intellectually smarter but is a symbol of wealth and a signal to others that one is a stakeholder in traditional educational systems and has substantially benefited from the status quo. In other words, an Ivy League degree is one of the ultimate markers of one's legitimate positionality within a particular social class group.

Social capital

Social Capital can be thought of as the "who you know" part of the adage shared previously and can be defined simply as *social networks and interpersonal connections, ranging from family and close friends to professional contacts and acquaintances*. With specific regard to social class, these networks and interpersonal relationships are so important because they may be used as a resource and may provide professional or economic opportunities. Think of a "social climber" and the effort a person puts into knowing the right people and accumulating these relationships. Other people are given and assigned *value* based on what they can contribute to the social climb. Consider, for example, how people learn about job opportunities. We may see a posting on social media, an online jobs site, or within the context of professional organizations. But Social Capital can also play a role here, in that job opportunities that are not publicized may be communicated less formally among friends and peers.

In some ECs in which professional networking is highly valued, developing Social Capital is a regular part of the job. People may be expected to go out for drinks after work, have important lunch meetings, attend meet-and-greet functions, or simply have business cards at the ready for any kind of interpersonal interaction that may arise. Of course, the concept of Social Capital has taken on new meanings in the age of social media. In the EC of social media platforms, the more traditional forms of investing in relationships in order to develop Social Capital, such as sharing business cards, are no longer viable and have been replaced by demands for followers. Social Capital in this instance is less about maintaining already-established relationships and more about regularly attracting new followers.

Cultural capital

To understand this final form of capital in the SCWM-R, let's extend the adage used previously. In addition to "what you know" (i.e., one form of Human Capital) and "who you know" (Social Capital), we would include whatever we find desirable, beautiful, pleasurable, or valuable. Turning again to that word *aesthetic*, Cultural Capital can be defined as *tastes and aesthetics that an individual has and continues to develop*. For our specific purposes here (that is, understanding social class as worldview), these tastes and aesthetics serve to reflect one's current or intended social class group. Cultural Capital may be demonstrated through our clothing, how we decorate our home, the food we eat (remember that *bougie* salad?), the leisure activities in which we participate, and the vacations we take (Liu, 2011).

Of course, different ECs place value on different forms of capital. Attending performing arts events or visiting art museums may be seen as Cultural Capital in an EC that values the arts. In another EC, expensive clothing and accessories or high-end cosmetics might be the valued commodities and a signal of someone's "good taste." In these examples, social class can be seen as something that is performed. Indeed, Cultural Capital can be seen as a form of "class signals" (Kraus et al., 2017) or "class practice" whereby people are motivated to show that they belong in a certain class by demonstrating the cultural aesthetics and tastes of that class group (Tournemaine & Tsoukis, 2008).

It is important to keep in mind that the subjective experience of Cultural Capital takes place in all of the objective social class positions that people occupy (e.g., upper, middle, lower). Returning to that image of the ladder, it may also be the case that people want to cultivate the Cultural Capital of a group believed to be "higher" than their particular social class – for example, by taking etiquette classes or engaging in behaviors that might be characterized as *bougie*. Alternatively, people may wish to cultivate the Cultural Capital of a group "lower" than their social class – for example, embracing a "shabby chic" decorating style. There are several terms for people who embrace cultural aesthetics that seem to contradict what their social class "is supposed to" value: Bobo (for "bourgeois Bohemian"; Brooks, 2010), silver-spoon hippie (Liu, 2011), and "trustafarian" (Griffin, 2010). These terms describe people who favor vintage or secondhand clothing, subcultural music, and alternative lifestyles.

Cultural Capital can also force a kind of commercialization and accumulation of experiences, or a form of "experiential money." In that sense, a vacation we take might becomes a valuable source of capital because we are motivated to accumulate important and valued vacation experiences. These experiences then can be used in interactions with others: to impress them, perhaps; to improve our social class positionality; or even to marginalize others who don't share our excellent taste and range of experiences. We can consider all of those social media posts we see as *performance* of Cultural Capital: vacations, excursions, day trips, and meals. And the height of Cultural Capital might involve being the first person to have a certain unique experience, or to discover a unique location, or to find the perfect off-the-beaten-path café.

Race in ECs; race and capital

Our discussion of ECs and capital provides an excellent opportunity to consider racial and structural inequality. As previously described, the SCWM-R contends that people in various ECs are expected to develop and maintain different forms of capital, but the challenges and inequities in developing those capitals frequently go unrecognized and unnamed within the ECs. As an example, consider two teenagers: one Black and one White, each from working-class ECs, and each fully committed to improving their intellect in their respective high schools and then attending college. This development of their Human Capital has to be understood within the larger contexts of structural racism and the ways that racism presents White people and BIPOC with different privileges and disadvantages with which to contend (Henry et al., 2020).

A great deal of education policy research focuses on the opportunity gap, which Darling-Hammond (2013) defines as the "cumulative differences in access to key educational resources that support learning at home and at school" (p. 77). This body of research has amply demonstrated that opportunities to develop such capital are unevenly distributed in the population and are less accessible for BIOPC than for White students (Welner & Carter, 2013; Darling–Hammond, 2004; Patrick et al., 2020; Sagauro Seminar, 2016), and these disparities begin as early as the prekindergarten years (Barnett & Lamy, 2013; Valentino, 2018).

Indeed, structural racism and classisms intersect in ways that create significant barriers, even in seemingly simple acts such as getting oneself to school. While the White student in this example may experience problems related to transportation, poorly paved roads, and the aging physical plants of their schools because of their socioeconomic positionality, they at least have the advantage of knowing they are not experiencing these problems because of their race. Students who are BIPOC do not have that advantage, which can readily be seen as a relatively small experience in their cumulative experience of internalized oppression and racial trauma (Awad et al., 2019; French et al., 2020; Sibrava et al., 2019).

Ladders and scaffolds

In Chapter 1, we discussed the ladder tool used to measure Subjective Social Status (Adler et al., 2000), and we refer to that tool a few times in this chapter. The ladder is a helpful metaphor in that it reflects cultural beliefs that social classes are linear and hierarchical, with the poor and working classes occupying the bottom rungs and upper-middle and upper classes occupying the higher rungs. However, as Will has suggested elsewhere (Liu, 2011), the metaphorical ladder image is limited in the sense that an actual ladder has just two "feet" upon which it stands. Rather than envision those in the most wealthy social classes as existing on the highest rungs of a ladder, he says, we should instead see them as existing on a multi-footed (and, hence, much more stable) scaffold.

For this scaffold metaphor, it's helpful to think of actual construction scaffolding in front of a building. Each of the individual "feet" of the scaffold represents a different kind of resource from which wealthier people can draw and use to continually reinforce their wealthy status and positionality. By "positionality" here we mean their status relative to other people. People born into intergenerational wealth are greeted by a scaffold where money is one of many important resources they already have. This wealth might confer an additional resource upon them: time, which they can use to their benefit – for example, by investing deeply into leisure and lifestyle matters. Other resources from which they can draw might include their relationships, their frequently reinforced positionalities, or even their material possessions. These resources generally protect them from macro–level economic phenomena such as recessions.

In contrast to those who benefit from such a scaffold, people who are not wealthy live and premise their upward mobility on the metaphorical ladder. The ladder, having only two feet, provides fewer resources for many of these individuals and families, perhaps the most important of which is paid employment. An economic downturn that causes someone to lose their job quickly makes the ladder unstable, and those depending on that job for upward mobility are simply at a loss. Moreover, the data on economic recessions show that for many families of Color who are not born into wealthy scaffolds, recessions hit hard and deeply (Mcintosh et al., 2020). For many of these families, their resource pool is shallow, easily depleted, and not quickly regenerated, and the economic shock can linger for generations. These economic downturns compound already-existing structural and institutional inequities and create more inequity from which it is harder to recover.

Inequality, gravity, and mobility: a helpful analogy

Most Americans agree that economic inequality is a significant problem in the United States, with 61% in one study indicating that "too much" inequality exists (Horowitz et al., 2020). Of those pointing to too much inequality, almost all believed some systemic change was needed, with 14% thinking the country's economic system should be "completely rebuilt," 67% saying that major changes were needed to address the problem, and 14% indicating minor changes were needed. The data reported here were collected before COVID-19 hit, and there is widespread agreement that the pandemic has worsened inequality on a number of fronts (Adams-Prossl et al., 2020; Perry et al., 2021; Stevenson, 2020).

Consider just two ways of measuring inequality: income inequality (the amount of income earned by a household) and wealth inequality (the amount of overall wealth held by a household). In terms of income inequality, in 2018, slightly more than half of all household income in the United States was earned by the top-earning 20% of households (Horowitz et al., 2020). Wealth inequality is a substantially more uneven metric, and in 2013, the richest 20% of households owned almost 90% of wealth (Desilver, 2015). And, again, keep in mind these are pre-COVID numbers.

Another point to keep in mind is that we can't talk about income and wealth inequality without also considering race and ethnicity, what Traub et al. (2017) starkly call the "asset value of Whiteness." Research on the racial wealth gap indicates that, on average (and before the COVID pandemic), White Americans held five times as much wealth as Latinx households and eight times as much wealth as Black households (Bhutta et al., 2020). This wealth inequality persists even when factoring in college enrollment, full-time employment, and spending patterns (Traub et al., 2017). And as Shapiro et al. (2013, 2019) point out, wealth inequality is highly complex and involves factors ranging from employment, retirement, credit and lending, and tax policy to housing, education, and criminal justice practices.

How do we make sense of these findings? How do inequality and economic mobility relate to one another, and how do we account for racial disparities therein? These questions become especially important when we consider the research finding that most Americans overestimate the degree of mobility that is actually achieved in our society (Kraus & Tan, 2015). Perhaps you'll find an analogy created by Will – involving the launching of the Space Shuttle – to be a helpful way to think about how the EC of American capitalism exerts influence on people's chances of mobility.

Consider how Earth's rotation and the forces of gravity keep people and objects grounded on the planet. Launching the Shuttle into space (that is, moving upward) runs counter to these forces and is the exact opposite of what these forces "want." Being on the ground/launch pad is the normal state of affairs and moving upward requires a tremendous amount of energy in the form of fuel. Most of that fuel is used in the very earliest stages of the launch when centripetal forces and gravity are most actively acting against upward movement. The engines are only turned off in the highest altitudes of flight, where gravitational forces are no longer a threat. In orbit, everything is simply easier to do and requires less energy.

Now consider that upward economic mobility is what our culture says it "wants" for all of us. Indeed, this upward mobility is the stated ideology of our meritocratic society: that economic success is almost guaranteed if one works hard enough. However, as an economic system, capitalism is most successful when many people stay in the lower levels of the economic system where they can be a relatively cheap source of labor. As was true for the Space Shuttle fighting gravity, moving upward in the socioeconomic system requires a tremendous amount of energy, and capitalism actually provides little of the necessary fuel. In other words, it provides few specific or material supports for that goal.

For the launch of the Space Shuttle, we understand explicitly that gravitational forces work against its upward trajectory. But in our economic system, matters are much less explicit. In fact, the invisible gravity of marginalization and inequity directly prohibits upward mobility, but the culture claims that upward mobility is possible and expected. To be in the 90% of Americans who are outside the protected bubble of wealth and affluence, this is the conflicting duality and tension that marks the lived experience of most of us. To state it more bluntly, we are told that being American means working hard and diligently within an economic system that has no interest or investment in our upward mobility.

This Space Shuttle analogy, of course, is not a perfect one. It doesn't explain all the complexities of upward mobility, nor the problems people may encounter as they try to move up the economic ladder. Our point here is not that individual effort and hard work don't matter. Of course they matter. Rather, we're suggesting that we can never lose sight of how much systemic energy is needed and how many resources are required for true economic mobility. And at any given time, if these resources are not available at the most critical times, upward mobility can be easily stalled if not completely thwarted. Unfortunately, there is no single point of investment that ensures that people can move upward. Rather, mobility comes from sustained and persistent resources, effort, and investments.

Engage with narratives and apply the theory

Read J.D. Scrimgeour's essay "A Good School" and Tina Fakhrid-Deen's "Ghetto Fabulous" and apply the SCWM-R to elements of those texts using the questions provided.

Box 3.1: Essay – "A Good School" by J.D. Scrimgeour

It's late afternoon, and the car battery dies while my family and I are at Salem Willows, the amusement park–turned–arcade down the road from Salem's power plant. I need to teach an evening class at Salem State College, and a long walk stretches ahead of me. An older couple that had driven over the bridge from Beverly for a bag of popcorn (a Willows' specialty) sees my distress and offers to drive me home. It's out of their way, but they do it cheerfully. On the ride, they find out I'm a professor at the college.

"Our niece went there. She loved it," the man tells me. I'm not surprised. Most people I meet in and around Salem speak appreciatively, even enthusiastically, about the college—either they went there, or they attended one of the theater productions, or they took a night class. This couple's niece had initially attended some well-known school and had disliked it. At Salem State she had small classes taught primarily by professors, not graduate students or part-timers. Her professors knew her name. "It's a good school," her aunt says.

A good school. It's a phrase I first heard in high school, when I was deciding where to apply to college. Thanks to good SAT scores, I received invitations from many colleges, most of which I had never heard: Case Western Reserve, Haverford, Bucknell. These, I was told—by my mother and by the savvy students in my Advanced Placement classes—were "good schools." If I wondered how someone who had never visited these schools could declare with utter certainty that they were "good," my doubts were erased by examining a guide to colleges, which labeled these schools "highly" or "extremely" competitive.

But what was a "good school"? I'm not sure the answer was clear to me as a prospective student or to the people writing the guides, for that matter. Only one impression was definite: a good school was one that people wanted to be in and where they felt a sense of importance. These schools weren't all the same; some promised personalities. If you attended Oberlin, you could feel that you were more of a free spirit than if you attended Amherst. Most important, though, if you went to a good school, you could take pride in it because it was a place that many people wanted to go to and not so many were accepted. To get accepted meant that you were among the chosen.

The Ivies seemed the most prestigious, and I ended up at Columbia University, drawn by the teeming streets of New York, and fascinated by James Simon Kunen's account of the 1968 student takeover in his *Strawberry Statement*. Of course, it also was important that Columbia had chosen me.

The distance between Columbia and Salem State at first seems too great to merit a comparison. Columbia is a world-renowned university, with a price to match. Salem State is an affordable public college in a state whose government cares little about public education. The students at Columbia are generally high achievers, graduates of top private and public high schools from accomplished and educated families. Many students at Salem State are first-generation college students from the less-affluent towns north of Boston. Many aspire to be nurses or high school teachers.

At Columbia, as at other good schools, it is presumed that one will get a "good education," another mushy phrase. According to the college guidebooks, a good education can be quantified: number of publications by faculty, number of books in the library. In its annual ranking of colleges, *U.S. News and World Report* weighs most heavily a school's endowment and the percentage of applicants it rejects. Just a smidgen of thought reveals how superficial and insignificant these numbers are. In my undergraduate education at Columbia, only a handful of professors inspired me. The most influential one I had only by accident, when he replaced a more famous professor who took a midsemester leave of absence after suffering a nervous breakdown. Did I count professors' publications before I enrolled in their classes? Did these publications make a whit of difference to my classroom experience? As an English major, I was one of fifty to a hundred students in the class. No one knew, or seemed to know, whether I showed up.

At some prestigious schools, underclassmen rarely get into classes with the prestigious faculty, and are taught instead by graduate students or adjuncts, part-timers who often shuttle among three or more campuses, collecting a pittance for their labor. Last summer, I had brunch with some faculty at Red's Diner, another Salem institution. Our waitress mentioned that she was thinking of going back to school and was considering Salem State. We got to talking. She had gone to Boston University for a year and hated it. Now in her midtwenties, she had recently returned from traveling and working in South America, and she had been taking courses at a community college. "And you know what?" she said, "I took two classes with the same teachers I had at B.U. And I was paying how much at B.U.?"

Mainly, a "good education" seems to mean that a diploma from the school makes you eligible for a "good job." *A good job.* A former student shares a bit of wisdom: in Los Angeles, everyone asks where you're from; in New York, everyone asks what you do; and around Boston, even if you're middle-aged, everyone asks what college you attended. When I think about how these attitudes affect my students, part of me is infuriated at the injustice. Yet another part of me thinks it is just as well. Why have our students strive to join that "good" world? If people are superficial enough to believe that money buys a better education, we want nothing to do with them anyway, do we? For the people I meet, like the older couple who gave me a lift, Salem State is a "good school." Is that enough?

What is the difference between Salem State and Columbia? At Salem State, accessible professors teach many of the students' courses, the classes are generally smaller than those at Columbia, and students aren't conferred a sense of entitlement upon graduation. Of course, there are also the other students: at a school like Columbia, which is devoted to accepting high achievers, one's classmates can be inspiring. It's not so easy to develop lifelong bonds at Salem State, where fellow students often rush to their cars after class to get to work or pick up their kids. I wish I could grant them the leisure to live the contemplative life that Columbia offers. Yet being among Salem State students, who often scramble to pay for school and try not always successfully, to squeeze in the time to go to classes, can be eye-opening and inspiring as well. During the latest war in Iraq, I asked a class—"How many of you have a friend or relative over there?" Only two students out of twenty did not raise their hands. I wonder what the numbers would be in a Columbia classroom.

I meet Tony on the back elevator in the library. He's in his midthirties, wearing the blue striped shirt of the maintenance workers, "Anthony" scripted in a white oval on the breast. We exchange hi's.

"You teach here, right?" he asks.

"Yeah, English."

"I took all my English classes," he says. "I'm a history major. I want to teach high school, go back and work with all those teachers I gave a hard time." He smiles.

"Good luck," I say.

When I get off the elevator, I'm still thinking about Tony. It isn't that he is so unusual—a full-time maintenance worker who is also a full-time student; it is that he is, it seems, so wonderfully typical here. The same person who is keeping the buildings up is taking classes in them. The gap between the blue-collar employees and students is so much smaller at Salem State than at all those schools I desired to attend. In this case, the employee and student were one and the same. And, better yet, he wanted to return to his community, to become a teacher.

What is there to say? I work at a good school.

Box 3.2: Essay – "Ghetto Fabulous" by Tina Fakhrid-Deen

Buying a house in the 'hood was a sociopolitical decision for me and my husband. I didn't want us to be the type of Black folks who get a little money and flee to the suburbs, away from our people. I live in Chicago. I was born on the west side of one of the most segregated cities in the nation, in the Jane Addams projects, a place commonly referred to as "the ghetto." It was a few miles west of downtown and close to everything imaginable—a prime location.

My family was poor, but resilient. We were no strangers to food stamps, roaches, and hallways that smelled of urine. We often had to eat those black-and-white-labeled generic brands and drink powdered milk, which I despised. I learned early on that sugar on a slice of bread or mixed with a glass of water made a tasty afternoon snack when peanut butter and jelly or Kool-Aid were unavailable.

I am proud of my roots and my complex identity, so it makes me sick when I hear people speak negatively about the ghetto, the place that I called home for many years. It is common to hear white and Black middle-class teens, in a skewed attempt to embrace hip-hop culture, say offensive things like, "Oh, my God, he is acting so ghetto," or, "Look at my big ghetto booty." Although the word "ghetto" refers to a section of the city densely populated by a certain minority group and was formerly where all Jewish people were dumped in some Eastern European countries (and later in Chicago and other big, American cities as well), the term is used quite differently now.

To those on the outside looking in, the term "ghetto" is now synonymous with being Black, dirty, attitudinal, ignorant, lazy, uneducated, and dangerous; it has taken on the same connotations that the term "nigger" historically has had. However different, they are both politically loaded terms used to denigrate poor Blacks, but to acknowledge that would be politically incorrect. "Ghetto" is the new code word for "low-income Black person." Whites won't acknowledge it because it feels too close to being racist, and middle-class Blacks won't acknowledge it because in their hearts, they know that using the word is a sad attempt to distance themselves from the lower class, to assimilate and be accepted by mainstream culture. It would be a public admission that poor Blacks are reduced to frightening caricatures, misunderstood by the majority of American society, still overtly oppressed.

I am ghetto. I love hip-hop, Ice Cube, and the Geto Boys. I have a big butt and snap my neck back and forth when I'm cussing someone out. I look good in cornrows and wild afros. I can do the "booty" dances with the best of them and I still say "ain't" to get my point across. I also have good parents, who always encouraged me to be the best and to speak my mind. As a result, I have a master's degree in education. No, my mama is not on welfare and yes, my father was present while I was growing up. I've never committed a crime, unless you count the time I stole a piece of bubble gum from 7-Eleven and returned it two minutes later out of guilt. I have a beautiful husband, not a "baby daddy." I've traveled to at least six different countries, studied abroad, and wear "ethnic" thrift-store dresses to work. I plan to teach our child Spanish and sign language. My ghetto identity is more than the latest booty-shake video, it is my foundation, and it reverberates through every facet of me—textured and rich. And no, I am not the exception.

My old neighborhood was ghetto. The scent of month-old chicken grease filled most homes, and stained blinds hung in the place of flowery curtains. There were scattered winos on the sidewalks, glass shards on the playground instead of wood chips, rampant petty crime, graffiti on the walls, and boarded-up windows on some apartments. There were also community centers where we could go and play board games and get juice and a "choke" sandwich (so damn dry you could choke eating them) until our parents got home. Hard-working parents worked several jobs to make ends meet and to provide a good, loving home for their families.

In school, we had spelling bees and learned Spanish in kindergarten. Caring adults with knowing eyes watched over us if our parents weren't around. We all knew each other's names and who to call when a child got out of line in the street. We were a community. My friends were ghetto. We did ghetto things, like drinking buttermilk with cookies and mixing Kool-Aid with sugar, giggling at the sour-sweet taste in our red-stained mouths. We played double dutch with a long extension cord while singing "take a peach, take a plum." Each time the jump rope hit one of us in the face, we had bitter fistfights, wind-milling with our eyes closed, hoping to make contact. At Halloween, we got yelled at or whipped for throwing eggs, not because it was childish and rude, but because we were screwing with the food supply. Some of us grew up to be construction workers, accountants, and teachers, while others became gang affiliates, hood rats, and drug dealers. Some moved out of the projects; some remain to this day. Some went off to college; others went off to prison. Regardless, we all shared the same history, cried the same tears, and mirrored the same struggle—withstanding poverty.

My family moved away from the projects when I was about six. We lived in the suburbs and then down South for a brief stint, but moved back to an urban area on the North Side of Chicago marked by many of the same characteristics as my former ghetto. Basically, we were still poor and struggling to survive. Upon returning to Chicago from college, I searched the city for housing. I drove back to my old neighborhood and, to my chagrin, found most of it had been torn down—shiny new town homes with skater boys stood in its place. It was now called "University Village," because a local university had bought up most of the property. Even the hospital where many of my friends and I were born had disappeared without a trace. It was almost as if we had never existed. It made my blood boil that all of those poor people had been displaced, and I wondered where they had gone. I blamed middle-class America and greedy developers. I accused the mayor and his cronies of turning a blind eye to what was happening in poor communities like mine.

I wanted to live in a place where all socioeconomic backgrounds were represented, no one above the other. I finally decided to move back to the North Side, for the diversity in ethnicities, cultures, and economic status. The local fruit market sold everything from *kimchi* and plantains to yucca and collard greens. *Elote* carts rolled down the street with hot ears of corn as often as ice cream trucks. Blue-collar and white-collar workers rode the el train together each morning. There were little coffee shops on several corners, adorned near the entrances by the occasional evening prostitute or homeless man. In my building lived a Jamaican drug dealer who often threw wild parties with the scent of cheeba oozing under the door; an alcoholic white man and his six-foot grocery cart–toting girlfriend, who fought like Ali and Frazier in a title bout; a spiritual Black vegetarian who swore that a cat's purr meant that it was going to attack her; a wiry ballerina who rented out her place every other month; some Eastern Europeans who spoke little English and managed the building; me and my mathematician husband; and an interracial couple who just seemed shady.

Slowly, many of the buildings in our area were converted to condos, the asking prices beyond ridiculous. The poor were being forced to move out, just like in my old neighborhood. They left a few Section Eight homes intact, for nostalgia's sake. Although gentrification came rapidly to our neighborhood, we weren't directly impacted until my mother (who lived down the street from us) was forced to move out of her tiny one-bedroom apartment when her rent jumped from $475 to $1,250 a month. Then our building changed hands, and the new owner threatened to almost double the rent for our modest one-bedroom. We all needed to move, and fast. My mother purchased her first home on the far South Side. Loving the diversity of the North Side, my husband and I tried to find another local property to purchase, but the price hikes were happening everywhere. We considered the suburbs, but quickly came back to reality. Why buy into the reverse white flight and allow upper-class whites to move back into the comforts and convenience of the city while we got stuck out in the boondocks, disconnected from everything we knew? So we did the most intelligent thing we could think of, we invested in Bronzeville, a historic South Side community.

During the great migration of the early 1900s, many Blacks emigrated from the South in hopes of landing industrial jobs in Chicago. Bronzeville was one of the only areas of the city that southern Blacks were allowed to live in. It is legendary for its sizzling-hot blues scene and notorious 47th St., a strip of juke joints, jazz cafes, restaurants, and hotels. This is where famous Black artists such as Billie Holiday and Ella Fitzgerald came to perform and stay when they had a gig in town. For years after its heyday, Bronzeville had been a poverty-stricken area filled with crime, despair, and little development. This was now one of the hot spots in the city to move to, because of its accessibility to downtown and the lakefront, and its affordable housing.

In a matter of days, we found a beautiful three-bedroom condo with a monthly mortgage in the same price bracket as our old apartment's rent increase. Set right on the main boulevard—named after a well-known Black civil rights leader—we could see all types of Black people walking up and down the street. This was the first time that I had been back in an all-Black area since my days in the ghetto and the South. It was exciting and wonderful, although I did miss the ethnic diversity of the North Side. There was a new Black-owned poetry cafe and a bank, and the alderwoman's office was less than a block away. It was rumored that a comedy club, performing arts theater, art gallery, and bookstore were in development on the next corner. Across the street, a sign boasted a new town-home development starting at $350,000. My husband and I thought that our neighbors were fabulous and incredibly nice. We had two lesbian pastors across the hall, three outgoing drug dealers, otherwise known as "pharmaceutical representatives," two PhD's, an ex-cop, a lawyer, and several high-powered businesswomen. We were all so close that it was like living in the dorms again.

I soon realized that I had somehow crossed over and was officially middle class. It was confusing, because I wasn't like the bourgeois Blacks who knew nothing about hard times and mocked the accursed lot of poor folks. I was different. I cared about civil rights for everyone. I didn't turn my nose up at the thought of eating pig feet or chitlins. I didn't fear that my property value would go down because poor folks lived next door. And I didn't refer to all less fortunate people, especially the expressive or thuggish-looking ones, as "ghetto." Then my whole reality changed. Within a week of our moving in to our new building there were two attempted robberies. I was four months pregnant and actually heard them kicking in my neighbor's door. A few weeks later, someone's car was broken into; then more robbery attempts in the coming months. I began to fear coming home late in the evening. As a pregnant woman in her third trimester, I was truly defenseless. My mind began betraying me. I questioned whether this neighborhood was good enough—safe enough—for me and my family. I feared the possibility of my child picking up broken crack vials in the neighborhood park during our afternoon strolls. I thought about sending our daughter to the substandard neighborhood schools. I thought about someone actually getting into our home, violating us and everything we've worked so hard for. I thought about moving—moving far away from crime, far away from my present reality, and even farther away from the ghetto we now lived in. It no longer felt like home—it felt like prison. It felt dangerous. It felt unforgiving. I felt like I was being punished for leaving the 'hood and coming back with a pot to piss in. I saw jealous eyes ogle me as I entered our six-foot gate, making sure it slammed behind me. I became resentful, fighting rage. I felt like a traitor.

I had become that middle-class asshole who moves in and pushes aside the poor residents, who are rightfully angry. They wanted the good life too. They wanted big-screen TVs and Jacuzzis like us. They wanted to feel important and respected, as we did. They also craved quality community resources for their families. No matter how I tried to frame it, I had become one of the powerful pawns in this gentrification game, with the poorest of Bronzeville being knocked clear off the board. Like magic, with our middle-class presence, the schools would begin to get better, more commercial development would find its way to the area, and politicians and policemen would make special visits to our condo association meetings to hear our concerns. We would complain about the crime and beg for the removal of it, of "them." My sensitivity for the wretched poor would wear thin. Ill feelings would grow between us and "them" until someone gave in and moved on. There could be no coexistence between the classes. We misunderstood and distrusted each other too much. There could be no community here.

Not until we stop to realize that we're all in this together. Not until I use my newfound middle-class power to advocate for the right to decent and affordable living for my new neighbors, here in Bronzeville. Not until I help them to advocate for themselves. Not until I realize that some of these residents don't want or need our middle-class handouts because they were doing just fine before we got here.

Not until I understand that many of these families are just like mine was back in the day, working hard and trying to keep food on the table. Not until I treat them as equals. Not until I stop being scared and open my mouth to say "hello" to the skeptical faces that eye me daily. Not until I recognize that the ones trying to rob us are just lost souls with no hope or heart left (that doesn't mean I won't keep calling the cops). Not until I get the resentment out of my heart.

The ghetto is a community filled with ups and downs, struggles and survivors and people sticking around hoping that things will get better. Being ghetto is so much more than a new catchphrase or a hip-hop song; it's an identity, a reflection of our economy, and a way of life. Just as hip-hop will be in my blood and spirit forever, so will the ghetto. I will transcend the box that us ghetto folks have been put into and create a new space. I will make people think before using the term "ghetto" to refer to any person, place, or thing. I will fight for the right to be ghetto, even when my back's against the wall, being violated by those I'm trying to stand up for. That's keeping it real—real ghetto. As a people, when one of us suffers, we all suffer. In my heart, I know that we ain't a true community until we take an honest look at each other and begin to embrace every part of our intricately woven culture. Black folks must get a handle on the crabs-in-a-barrel syndrome, and learn to stand strong, together.

Discussion questions/assignment prompts:

1   Scrimgeour describes two contexts in his essay which can be seen as ECs: the college where he is employed, and the university he attended. How are these ECs alike and different? What qualities are valued within each EC? How does Social Capital differ at each institution? How does the task of developing Human Capital differ in each EC? Make sure to use specific textual evidence.

2   How might students and families use the different meanings of "a good school" as a form of Cultural Capital?

3   Extend the metaphors of the "ladder" and the "scaffold" to the students and families described in Scrimgeour's essay.

4   Fakhrid-Deen describes having lived in several neighborhoods in Chicago: the West Side, then the suburbs, then an "urban area on the North Side," and ultimately Bronzeville on the South Side. Discuss these moves in terms of the comfort and discomfort of moving between different ECs as discussed in the chapter.

5   Fakhrid-Deen describes the micro-level ECs of her childhood and current neighborhoods in Chicago, and she also provides several examples of macro-level "sociopolitical" and cultural forces that impact those local ECs. Discuss the specific macro-level forces that she mentions and describe the kinds of influence they exert on neighborhoods and people. Use specific textual evidence.

6   Intersectionality Check-In: Provide some specific textual evidence showing where Fakhrid-Deen describes the intersectionality of social class and race.

7   Digital Spotlight: Review the three forms of Capital in the SCWM-R and discuss which one(s) shows up most frequently on social media? Why do you think that is? Are there differences between the various platforms (e.g., Instagram, TikTok)?

8   What's Your Story? When you were growing up, which of the three forms of Capital described here were most important to your family? Do you have experience with moving between ECs and sensing the shift in which forms of Capital were most valued?

References

Adams-Prossl, A., Golin, M., & Rauch, C. (2020). Inequality in the impact of the coronavirus shock: Evidence from real time surveys. *Journal of Public Economics, 189.* https://doi.org/10.1016/j.jpubeco.2020.104245

Adler, N.E., Epel, E.S., Castellazzo, G., & Ickovics, J.R. (2000). Relationship of subjective and objective social status with psychological and physiological functioning: Preliminary data in healthy, White women. *Health Psychology, 19*(6), 86–592. https://doi.org/10.1037/0278-6133.19.6.586

Andrews, D., & Sánchez, A.C. (2011). The evolution of homeownership rates in selected OECD countries: Demographic and public policy influences. *OECD Journal: Economic Studies, 2011*(1). http://dx.doi.org/10.1787/eco_studies-2011-5kg0vswqpmg2

Awad, G.H., Kia-Keating, M., & Amer, M.M. (2019). A model of cumulative racial-ethnic trauma among Americans of Middle Eastern and North African (MENA) descent. *American Psychologist, 74*(1), 76–87. https://doi.org/10.1037/amp0000344

Barnett, W.S., & and Lamy, C.E. (2013). Achievement gaps start early: Preschool can help. In P.L. Carter & K.G. Welner (Eds.), *Closing the opportunity gap: What America must do to give every child an even chance* (pp. 98–110). New York, NY: Oxford University Press.

Belle, D. (2006). Contested interpretations of economic inequality following Hurricane Katrina. *Analyses of Social Issues and Public Policy, 6*(1), 143–158. Publisher: Hoboken, NJ: Blackwell. https://doi.org/10.1111/j.1530-2415.2006.00111

Bhutta, N., Chang, A.C., Dettling, L.J., & Hsu, J.W. (2020, September 28). *Disparities in wealth by race and ethnicity in the 2019 survey of consumer finances.* Washington, DC: Federal Reserve System. www.federalreserve.gov/econres/notes/feds-notes/disparities-in-wealth-by-race-and-ethnicity-in-the-2019-survey-of-consumer-finances-20200928.htm

Brooks, D. 2010. *Bobos in paradise: The new upper class and how they got there.* New York, NY: Simon and Schuster.

Darling-Hammond, L. (2004). Inequality and the right to learn: Access to qualified teachers in California's public schools. *Teachers College Record, 106*(10), 1936–1966.

Darling-Hammond, L. (2013). Inequality and school resources: What it will take to close the opportunity gap. In P.L. Carter & K.G. Welner (Eds.), *Closing the opportunity gap: What America must do to give every child an even chance* (pp. 77–97). New York, NY: Oxford University Press.

Desilver, D. (2015). *The many ways to measure economic inequality.* Washington, DC: Pew Research Center. www.pewresearch.org/fact-tank/2015/09/22/the-many-ways-to-measure-economic-inequality/

French, B.H., Lewis, J.A., Mosley, D.V., Adames, H.V., Chavez-Dueños, N.Y., Chen, G.A., & Neville, H.A. (2020). Toward a psychological framework of radical healing for people of Color. *The Counseling Psychologist, 45*(1), 14–46. https://doi.org/10.1177/0011000019843506

Griffin, B. (2010). *The trustafarian handbook: A field guide to the neo-hippy lifestyle funded my mom and dad.* New York, NY: Simon and Schuster.

Henry, D.A., Cortés, L.B., & Votruba-Drzal, E. (2020). Black-White achievement gaps differ by family socioeconomic status from early childhood through early adolescence. *Journal of Educational Psychology, 112*(8), 1471–1489. https://doi.org/10.1037/edu0000439

Horowitz, J.M., Igielnik, R., & Kochhar, R. (2020, January 9). *Most Americans say there is too much economic inequality in the U.S., but fewer than half call it a top priority.* Washington, DC: Pew Research Center. www.pewresearch.org/social-trends/2020/01/09/most-americans-say-there-is-too-much-economic-inequality-in-the-u-s-but-fewer-than-half-call-it-a-top-priority/

Kraus, M.W., Park, J.W., & Tan, J.J.X. (2017). Signs of social class: The experience of economic inequality in everyday life. *Perspectives on Psychological Science, 12*(3), 422–435. https://doi.org/10.1177/1745691616673192

Kraus, M.W., & Tan, J.J.X. (2015). Americans overestimate class mobility. *Journal of Experimental Social Psychology, 58*, 101–111. http://dx.doi.org/10.1016/j.jesp.2015.01.005

Langner, T., & Schmidt, J. (2015). Is it really love? A comparative investigation of the emotional nature of brand and interpersonal love. *Psychology and Marketing, 32*(6), 624–634. https://doi.org/10.1002/mar.20805

Liu, W.M. (2011). *Social class and classism in the helping professions: Research, theory, and practice.* Thousand Oaks, CA: Sage Publications.

Markus, H.R., & Stephens, N.M. (2017). Editorial overview: Inequality and social class: The psychological and behavioral consequences of inequality and social class: A theoretical integration. *Current Opinion in Psychology, 18*, iv–xxi. https://doi.org/10.1016/j.copsyc.2017.11.001

Mcintosh, K., Moss, E., Nunn, R., & Shambaugh, J. (2020, February 22). *Examining the Black-White wealth gap.* Washington, DC: The Brookings Institution. www.brookings.edu/blog/up-front/2020/02/27/examining-the-black-white-wealth-gap/

Patrick, K., Socol, A., & Morgan, I. (2020, January 9). *Inequities in advanced coursework: What's driving them and what leaders can do.* Oakland, CA: The Education Trust. https://edtrust.org/resource/inequities-in-advanced-coursework/

Perry, B.L., Aronson, B., & Pescosolido, B.A. (2021). Pandemic precarity: COVID-19 is exposing and exacerbating inequality in the American heartland. *PNAS, 118*(8), 1–6. https://doi.org/10.1073/pnas.2020685118

Sagauro Seminar. (2016). *Closing the opportunity gap.* Cambridge: Harvard Kennedy School. http://theopportunitygap.com/

Shapiro, T., Meschede, T., & Osoro, S. (2013). *The roots of the widening racial wealth gap: Explaining the Black-White economic divide.* Waltham, MA: Brandeis/Heller School/IASP. https://heller.brandeis.edu/iere/pdfs/racial-wealth-equity/racial-wealth-gap/roots-widening-racial-wealth-gap.pdf

Shapiro, T., Santos, J., & Stewart, S. (2019). *The Black-White racial wealth gap.* Waltham, MA: Brandeis/Heller School/IASP. www.tminstituteldf.org/

Sibrava, N.J., Bjornsson, A.S., Pérez Benítex, A.C.I., Moitra, E., Weisberg, R.B., & Keller, M.B. (2019). Posttraumatic stress disorder in African American and Latinx adults: Clinical course and the role of racial and ethnic discrimination. *American Psychologist, 74*(1), 101–116. https://doi.org/10.1037/amp0000339

Stevenson, B. (2020). *The initial impact of COVID-19 on labor market outcomes across groups and the potential for permanent scarring.* Washington, DC: Brookings/Hamilton Project. www.brookings.edu/wp-content/uploads/2020/07/Stevenson_LO_FINAL.pdf

Tournemaine, F., & Tsoukis, C. (2008). Relative consumption, relative wealth, and growth. *Economics Letters, 100*(2), 314–316. https://doi.org/10.1016/j.econlet.2008.02.018

Traub, A., Sullivan, L., Meschede, T., & Shapiro, T. (2017). *The asset value of whiteness: Understanding the racial wealth gap.* New York, NY: Demos. www.demos.org/sites/default/files/publications/Asset Value of Whiteness_0.pdf

Valentino, R. (2018). Will public pre-K really close achievement gaps? Gaps in prekindergarten quality between students and across states. *American Educational Research Journal, 55*(1), 79–116. https://doi.org/10.3102/0002831217732000

Welner, K.G., & Carter, P.L. (2013). Achievement gaps arise from opportunity gaps. In P.L. Carter & K.G. Welner (Eds.), *Closing the opportunity gap: What America must do to give every child an even chance* (pp. 1–10). New York, NY: Oxford University Press.

Yosso, T. (2005). Whose culture has capital? A critical race theory discussion of community cultural wealth. *Race Ethnicity and Education, 8*(1), 69–91. https://doi.org/10.1080/1361332052000341006

4 Development of the Social Class Worldview (lessons, levels, and lenses)

Component 2 of the SCWM-R

Accompanying Essays: Courtney Eldridge, "Thanks, but No Thanks"; Anne E. Noonan, "Stink Tree"

Check your comprehension

- ECs are defined as environments or contexts that do the following. (1) Help us make sense of how social class operates in the world. (2) Value and expect certain forms of capital from us with regard to social class. (3) Determine what we need to do to maintain our social class standing.
- The SCWM-R depicts three specific forms of capital: Human Capital, Social Capital, and Cultural Capital. Racism and other forms of structural inequity can thwart the development of the valued forms of capital.
- ECs exist at "micro" levels (such as neighborhood or workplace) and at more "macro" levels (such as a country's overall economic system).
- The Worldview is the lens through which we make sense of all the multiple and interconnected aspects of social class, classisms, and other forms of structural inequities.

What do you think?:

1 Briefly consider the following questions. Is the world basically fair? Does everything happen for a reason? Are people basically good? Do people get what they deserve? Are strangers simply friends we haven't met yet? Are all people born with equal opportunities? Are life circumstances the result of individual behavior and will or are they mostly the work of a force larger than ourselves?

2 What lessons have your family members passed on to you with regard to social class or classism? How were those messages delivered and by whom?

3 How are tattoos and other body modifications viewed in your family? Are they seen as an interesting and edgy form of artistic or self-expression or a way to pay tribute, say, to a deceased loved one? Or are they considered "trashy" and something to be avoided?

4 What's considered the standard and appropriate attire for most situations? Covered necklines, polo-style shirts, khaki pants, sneakers, or boat shoes? Are yoga pants acceptable in all situations? Do button-down shirts always have to be pressed and tucked in? How do we determine what clothing is "classy" and what clothing is "basic"?

DOI: 10.4324/9780429317606-5

What does it mean to have a worldview?

Welcome to the heart of the SCWM-R, the component that examines the development of a Social Class Worldview through a focus on *lessons, levels,* and *lenses.* In its most basic sense, having a worldview means exactly what the word suggests: a way of seeing and understanding the world. Recall how in Chapter 3 we asserted that ECs can exist at micro-levels (e.g., our neighborhoods) and at more macro-levels (e.g., the capitalist economic system of the United States). Similarly, when we discuss the worldview, the term "world" can mean spaces and contexts quite near to us, as well as spaces and contexts that exist further away from us. To use the terminology of Urie Bronfenbrenner's ecological systems theory (Bronfenbrenner & Morris, 2006), "world" can mean forces such as family and peers who are quite close to us as individuals (what Bronfenbrenner calls the *microsystem*), less immediate but still influential forces such as neighborhood wealth or poverty (the *exosystem*), and larger-scale forces such as the strength of the national economy (the *macrosystem*).

General definitions of worldview tend to focus on the nature of reality (Koltko-Rivera, 2004), people's "ability to ask and reflect on 'big questions'" (Taves et al., 2018), or people's overall beliefs and assumptions about the world. The way you answered the first "What Do You Think?" question might shed some light on your own worldview, in this more general and philosophical way. Now let's turn our attention to the more specific idea of a Social Class Worldview and the Worldview component of the SCWM-R.

In previous work, Will has provided this definition of *Social Class Worldview*: the *beliefs, attitudes, and values that individuals use to interpret their economic and social class situations and conditions* (Liu, 2011). These beliefs, attitudes, and values influence the way we come to see the self, the world in general, other people, and our relationships with those people. Thus, the Social Class Worldview is also a composite of the biases, distortions, and preferences we have about economic issues and inequities. The SCWM-R allows us to see where these biases may come from and how they extend into the rest of our psychological worldview. You may have already realized that this second component of the SCWM-R has a reciprocal relationship with the first component. Recall that one of the functions of ECs is to help develop our Social Class Worldviews. In turn, our Social Class Worldviews help us to continue understanding the capital demands exerted upon us by the various ECs in which we operate. Within these ECs, we also experience the impact of race and racism, as well as gender and sexism and our worldviews about social class overlap with our worldviews about race, gender, and other important identities/social constructs.

Lessons: development of the Social Class Worldview through socialization messages

A major way that Social Class Worldviews develop is through *Socialization Messages,* defined as *explicit or implicit lessons or communications about the way social class operates, and about what is expected of us as "classed beings"* (Liu, 2011). These Socialization Messages come from a variety of sources: the ECs within which we operate, of course, and also from family members, friends, and peers, social media, popular media, and advertising. These lessons tell us about what work and effort mean, how or whether one's race, or gender, or experiences of racism and sexism are relevant to social mobility. Socialization Messages teach us about cultural belief systems – for example, meritocracy (the belief that success comes from ability and hard work) or egalitarianism (the belief that all people are equal and should be treated accordingly). Socialization Messages also have a role to play in climbing the so-called social class ladder. If we aspire to become a member of a social class group that is higher than our current social class, we may pay especially close attention to Socialization Messages from members of that social class about what is appropriate and desirable and also what is expected of members of that class.

Socialization Messages can be explicit or implicit. An explicit Socialization Message about social class is one in which social class is front and center or is directly mentioned. Examples might include the following.

- *If you work hard, economic success will come to you.*
- *You have to spend money to make money.*
- *One person's trash is another person's treasure.*
- *Keep your head down and don't make trouble.*
- *Money isn't everything . . . but it helps.*
- *Avoid being in debt.*
- *There is good debt (investments) and bad debt.*
- *Pay your bills on time.*
- *You might have money, but that doesn't mean you have class.*
- *Waste not, want not.*
- *You get what you pay for.*

Implicit Socialization Messages, on the other hand, are those that have a social class or classism theme to them but don't directly mention or allude to social class. Consider your answer to the "What Do You Think?" question about tattoos. For example, a young adult or even an older person mentioning a desire for a tattoo might not hear the word "trashy" mentioned but might instead hear a more vague message such as, "We don't do that in this family," or, "That's not how I want you presenting yourself to the world."[1]

Of course, implicit messages may also be more silent – that is, acted out but never remarked upon. Imagine a parent and young child running errands in town one day. They see someone who appears to be homeless asking for money, and the parent either gives the person some money or speeds up their pace and ignores the person. What is the Socialization Message here? In one scenario, the child is being socialized, quietly, to treat people in need or with fewer financial resources as worthy of respect or assistance. In the other scenario, the child is being socialized to fear or keep away from people in need or treat them as though they are invisible.

Now let's overlay race onto this example. Imagine that the parent and child are White, and sometimes they encounter a homeless person who is White, and other times the homeless person is Black. Does the parent react differently depending on the person's race? Does the child begin to notice, for example, that the parent stops and gives homeless White people money more frequently than they do with homeless Black people? In this case, a Socialization Message about social class is intricately woven together with information about race and demonstrates the intersectionality of social class and race.

For another example, imagine a child being exposed to different Socialization Messages about people of different races or ethnicities and about different displays of materialism.

---

1   To take this tattoo example even further, consider that term "tramp stamp." Since the word "tramp" can have both social class meaning and sexual meaning, might the term "tramp stamp" represent the intersection of social class and sexuality?

We think it's safe to say that showing off belongings or being ostentatious and flashy can happen in any ECs and environment, even if the items being displayed differ because they cost different amounts. But compare the possible reactions to a White family posting pictures of themselves dripping in gold vs. a Latinx family posting pictures of a *Quiceañera* celebration. How might the developing worldview be shaped by a reaction, in the first instance of "not my style, but good for them; they earned it" vs. a reaction in the second instance that the dresses are too fancy ("ghetto fabulous") or that the family is living beyond their means. In these hypothetical examples, the simple idea of "deservingness" is not just "class-ified" but is also racialized.

Upward mobility bias

For most people, the strongest Socialization Messages to which they are exposed are related to meritocracy and *moving-up* social classes. Think about what messages you may have received growing up about the importance of climbing that socioeconomic ladder. In the ECs in which you were raised, was there an assumption that everyone wants to keep climbing that ladder? Will has described this assumption as a form of Upward Mobility Bias (UMB; Liu, 2011). This particular bias affects almost everyone, and it can appear in explicit ways and also in more subtle, implicit ways. Basically, the UMB is the expectation that everyone around us is interested in some form of social class movement toward increased wealth, higher levels of education, or more prestigious jobs and occupations. And, as a Socialization Message, the UMB acts as a gauge for how similar we might be with others.

When we first interact with someone, our UMB might kick into gear as we subtly ask about where they went to school and what they currently do for work. These inquiries allow us to situate ourselves in comparison to them. Are they on the same or similar trajectory as we are? Are we compatible as friends? Do we see the world similarly or differently? If we ourselves wish for economic mobility, the UMB is also active when we interact with people without that mobility ambition – that is, a person with no interest in furthering their education, being promoted at work, accumulating more wealth, or moving to a "better" neighborhood. In this case, the questions we ask to assess mobility typically fall flat, and we might decide that we don't have much in common.

An interesting exception to the UMB involves the people Schor (1999) called *downshifters*. You may recall that in Chapter 3, we mentioned similar terms such as Bobos, silver-spoon hippies, and trustafarians. Downshifters are people – usually White people – who were in occupations such as finance and banking but left these occupations after deciding that they had enough of climbing the social class ladder and enough of their own and others' UMB. Instead of being a Wall Street hedge fund manager, for example, a person might now be an artisanal goat cheese maker in upstate New York. Downshifters such as this might valorize their new rural settings, as well as their newfound *blue-collar* jobs. To some extent, they are choosing to live in ways that seem opposed to the Socialization Messages with which they were raised.

However, while the downshifters might associate with the farmers in the area, they are not truly blue-collar workers, nor have they left their wealth behind. These people were able, after all, to *choose* this new life. Instead, they manage their wealth passively and on the side. They simply see themselves as having shifted out of their high-paced corporate world and shifted into this different EC. But because they still have access to their tremendous wealth (that is, what they own minus what they owe), they've not really exited from their previous EC, nor do they fully exist in their current one. They have not erased or undone the Socialization Messages with which they were raised.

Rather, their wealth allows them to seemingly situate themselves between two ECs, all the while really existing within their still wealthy EC. Their proximity to the farmers in their area adds to their uniqueness and lifestyle and adds value to their products. But in the way that some graduates of Harvard or Yale always manage to squeeze in that pedigree, the new farmer might feel compelled to remind people that they *chose* to do this work and *chose* to take on this different lifestyle. As mentioned, downshifters tend to be White, and one of the benefits of Whiteness is the ability to downshift and to move between these spaces without any dire consequences.

Turning back to Will's metaphor of the scaffold described in Chapter 3 (Liu, 2011), downshifters can be seen as existing within a wealthy scaffolded existence, one suffused with the structural advantages and positionality that come with White wealth. They can invest in multiple forms of resources (in two ECs, in two groups of people, in two lifestyles, in two ways to spend time) without the fear of losing their positionality. And whether we use the term downshifter, silver-spoon hippie, Bobo, or trustafarian, the basic elements are clear. People of some wealth and means have decided that they don't want to live a particular wealthy lifestyle or don't want to be associated with it outright. Instead, they have invested in a more rustic, supposedly less conventional, or seemingly more authentic lifestyle.

Levels: shifting awareness and consciousness about social class and classism

Sometimes, at this point in learning about the SCWM-R, students put the brakes on and ask whether we might be overreacting. Could we be overstating the importance of social class? Sometimes they tell us that they truly "never give this stuff any thought." Conversely, other students have told us that learning about the model turns on a light switch in their minds or that a secret language is being decoded for them. As one student recently indicated in a written assignment, "The SCWM-R puts into words the language I had been lacking and concepts I couldn't explain but knew and have known very well my whole life." Further, we even hear comments such as, "Wow, I actually see social class *everywhere* right now." To be sure, one of the most interesting aspects of teaching undergraduate and graduate students about the psychology of social class (or working with clients, or hearing research participants talk about social class) is the variation in levels of awareness and consciousness that people have about their social class experiences.

This "levels" part of the second component of the SCWM-R has a more formal name: Social Class and Classism Consciousness (SCCC) (Liu, 2011). SCCC involves the extent to which we understand (or don't) that we exist in a social class system. The model depicts three broad levels or domains: *No/Low Social Class Consciousness, Social Class Self-Consciousness, and Social Class Consciousness.* We will explain each of these levels in turn, using an example of a college student named Samuel, who is a first-generation college student and a member of the honors program at his university where he double-majors in psychology and sociology.

The first level in the SCCC is the *No/Low* Social Class Consciousness level in which people are largely unaware of social class in their lives. They may not completely lack awareness, but they have not developed a complex or sophisticated understanding of how social class operates. Certainly, they have received Socialization Messages from others in their ECs, but those lessons remain largely unquestioned. Perhaps our students who claim to "never give this stuff any thought" are situated in this level of the SCCC. Turning to our fictional example, Samuel has learned from family members to believe in the idea of meritocracy: that those who work hard will enjoy economic success. But his family members may have never explored the cultural, systemic, and structural forces and privileges that allow some people to succeed without real effort. As Samuel accumulates more social class experiences outside of the family and spends time in other ECs (such as college) though, he may begin to question and challenge this whole notion of meritocracy, even if he remains unable to fully understand its limitations or articulate those limitations to others.

When you imagined Samuel, who did you see? Did you see a White person or someone who is BIPOC? How might his race be related to his level of Social Class Consciousness? How might his race, or his experiences with racism, impact how he thinks about meritocracy? Further, think about people who say they "never give this [social class] stuff any thought." Does not having to think about social class reflect a certain amount of class privilege? And considering the interconnectedness of social class inequality and race, would White racial privilege factor in here as well? Could never giving "this stuff" any thought also reflect White racial privilege? Could it be the case that White people are able to choose if and when they think about social class but BIPOC less frequently have such a choice?

At the next level, Social Class *Self*-Consciousness, Samuel may begin to develop a self-consciousness about – that is, an acute sensitivity to – his ECs, social class experiences, and the ways that others perceive him with regard to social class. However, Samuel's evolving sensitivity still lacks complexity, and he remains unable to decipher how power, privilege, and inequality operate. Stated more simply, Samuel knows that "something is up," but he doesn't know exactly what. As is the case for other people at this level, Samuel's focus is largely on himself, and this self-focus allows him to turn inward, explore what he knows about social class and classism, and try to make sense of it all. And, of course, race and racism come into play here as well. How might Samuel's race intersect with his social class self-consciousness? How might he interact differently with those he perceives as racially similar or dissimilar?

With regard to the myth of meritocracy, at this level, Samuel looks for ways to justify the perspective that people who get ahead are talented and hardworking. Any new information that challenges the idea of meritocracy is uncomfortable for him, and he may resort to strategies of dismissal, denial, or minimization. Samuel's discomfort may turn to despair, causing him to give up trying to understand all the complexities of social class. He may even conclude that, for the most part, the world is just and fair, and people get what they deserve.

Samuel might recognize and acknowledge that economic inequality exists, but he may conclude that inequality is a natural part of the U.S. economic system. He may further conclude that those who fail to succeed within the system do so because of their own individual-level deficiencies rather than because of systemic or structural barriers. Alternatively, he may try harder to understand large-scale, class-related issues, such as the experience of living in poverty. From the relative safety of this intellectualization, Samuel may begin to envision large-scale social changes needed to eliminate poverty at a macro-level. However, he may again become frustrated when he realizes how stubborn and entrenched poverty can be. Unable to envision any meaningful small steps that can chip away at poverty, he may return to a position of blaming the poor for being poor.

In the final level, Social Class Consciousness, the attention to and exploration of social class evolve from a focus on merely the self to a focus on the self, on others, and on society as a whole. Samuel may become curious about how he, as a social classed being, influences other people, and he may begin to think deeply about how race figures into the equation. He may come to see that his interpersonal interactions are related to macro-level problems of inequality, and he may seek meaningful ways to positively impact the lives of others. He may choose to donate money or to volunteer at a local homeless shelter or feeding program. He may even become involved in advocacy or explore graduate programs in social inequality. Continuing on this path, Samuel may develop a full-bodied understanding of his role in, and relationship to, inequality, classisms, and racism. He won't kid himself that change will take place overnight, but he will begin to see that very real impact is possible.

Although we won't spend much time discussing them, you should know that nested within these three levels are ten specific "statuses," as indicated in Table 4.1. These statuses provide a deeper dive – a more specific and nuanced understanding of the shifts that we undergo as we accumulate class-relevant experiences and continue to interact with other people and with various contexts and social structures. In Samuel's story, we didn't name the statuses, but we did describe his progression through them. Statuses within the No/ Low Consciousness level are *Unawareness, Status Position Salience,* and *Questioning.* Statuses within the Self-Consciousness level are *Exploration and Justification, Despair, The World Is Just,* and *Intellectualized Anger and Frustration.* Finally, the statuses within the consciousness level are *Reinvestment, Engagement,* and *Equilibration.* Those wanting this deeper understanding of the statuses will find Appendix A useful, which provides definitions of each status, as well as descriptions of how people in a particular status see themselves, peers, other people, and society as a whole.

Perhaps you have noticed in Samuel's story a hierarchical progression from less sophisticated to more sophisticated ways of thinking about social class. But you have also probably noticed that he engaged in some shifting back and forth among the SCCC levels and statuses. Indeed, the SCCC levels and statuses in this model do not represent a classical stage model in which people gain competence in a task at a given level and are then able to progress to the next level and take on new tasks. Rather, the levels and statuses represent a series of relatively predictable shifts in worldview that we *may* experience as we walk through life as a classed being and/or as situations demand.

For example, a person who has always believed in an "even playing field" when it comes to economic success may have a difficult time holding onto that belief when

Table 4.1: Social Class and Classism Consciousness Model: Levels and Statuses

No/Low Social Class Consciousness
    Unawareness
    Status Position Saliency
    Questioning
Social Class Self-Consciousness
    Exploration and Justification
    Despair
    The World is Just
    Intellectualized Anger and Frustration
Social Class Consciousness
    Reinvestment
    Engagement
    Equilibration

confronted with data indicating that the wealthiest 1% of Americans hold more than a third of the nation's overall wealth (Shapiro et al., 2013). Similarly, a person who believes that race is irrelevant may struggle to explain the various racial inequities discussed in Chapter 3. An increasingly complex level of understanding will be necessary to make sense of these realities, and people may experience shifts in worldview similar to what Samuel experienced. They may make a relatively smooth and linear progression, or they may experience a more jagged progression, every once in a while dipping back to an earlier status. And of course, it's always possible that they will maintain a relatively less sophisticated Social Class Worldview.

It is important to recognize that developing a consciousness about social class and classism adds an additional layer of complexity for people who are BIPOC who are also trying to come to terms with race and racism, and make sense of their lives, their relationships, and how they exist in a racialized society. And the challenge is not merely a cognitive one. The varying forms of Social Class Consciousness described here intersect with racial identity, ideas about acculturation, and experiences with racial trauma and microaggressions (Bryant-Davis & Ocampo, 2006; French et al., 2020; Liu et al., 2019; Mosley et al., 2020; Sue et al., 2019). In these ways, Social Class Consciousness and experiences with classisms may create additional forms of psychological distress and conflict as the individual tries to reconcile and make sense of racism and classisms. Indeed, while many White people may see classisms and racism as distinct and separate, for most BIPOC, racism and classisms are forged together in daily lived experiences.

Lenses: beliefs, attitudes, and values

As we hope you recall, the SCWM-R defines the Social Class Worldview as a set of beliefs, attitudes, and values that individuals use to interpret their economic and social class situations and conditions. Before we describe those beliefs, attitudes, and values, we offer up the metaphor of a camera lens. At the time this chapter was being written, the most recent version of the iPhone is the iPhone 12, with release of an iPhone 13 (or 12S) on the horizon. Each device has multiple camera lenses (or modes/systems), each with a specific use. When users want a certain image or certain effect, they decide which specific lens to use.

Similarly, when it comes to the Social Class Worldview, the SCWM-R contends that there are three predominant ways that people view social class – that is, three predominant lenses through which they see and come to understand social class: materialism and possessions, class–congruent behaviors, and lifestyle. Certain people may habitually prefer a certain lens over the other lenses. Or it might be the case that certain contexts might dictate which lens to use. Just as with the iPhone, when one lens is in operation, the other lenses still exist, but they exist in the background until called upon again.

The lens of materialism and possessions

Think of the most materialistic person you know. Was it easy to conjure that person? What specific behaviors does that person exhibit that made you think of them? How would you define materialism? You probably have your own sense of what that term means, and definitions can be found in the literature of various academic disciplines: economics, philosophy, religious studies, and of course psychology. For purposes of our discussion here, we offer this definition from a study examining the link between materialism and well-being: "values, goals, and associated beliefs that center on the importance of acquiring money and possessions that convey status" (Dittmar et al., 2014).

For some people, possessions are not just important but are perhaps *the most important* aspect of life. People for whom this is true may primarily see the self, the world, other people, and even relationships in terms of possessions. That is, their possessions are extensions of themselves, and people who are prone to materialism expect others to "ooh and aah" over what they own. Materialistic people want others to see them fused with their possessions, and they may believe that this fusing or combination actually represents their full self. No wonder they can get profoundly upset when people don't get excited about a new possession they have because this person experiences it as a rejection of them.

Additionally, those who are materialistic may evaluate and judge others in terms of clothing, designer labels, cars, homes, and even bikes (Liu, 2011), and conversations frequently revolve around things, objects, and possessions. Because they see themselves as fused with their belongings, they assume others are the same. Additionally, such people are acutely aware of others' evaluations of them and are likely to self-monitor and be constantly sensitive to self-presentation and their own display of material things and objects. In these ways, it's not hard to imagine that people using this lens on a regular basis may experience lower levels of well-being.

Materialism and possessions certainly can be used to exhibit one's social class position; therefore, the cultivation (or curating) of specific objects takes on a level of importance and attention. Materialism and possessions can also represent a way to cope with stresses and conflicts in relationships or intrapsychically (Rice et al., 2020). Thus, *having things* or the act of buying things can reflect a particular way to manage psychological stress. Materialism frequently takes on negative connotations such as being superficial or lacking impulse control, and for some individuals, those interpretations are accurate. Yet we also have to consider that *having things* can also be a way to signal our achievements and show others that we are successful. Distinguishing between these two forms of materialism is especially important when we consider that material possessions may take on different meanings for people in different racial groups.

The lens of class-congruent behaviors

Another lens in the Social Class Worldview involves social class–based behaviors, and those who favor this lens see the self, the world, other people, and even relationships in these terms. Recall that earlier we suggested that Socialization Messages might be implicit or explicit. The lens of class-congruent behaviors specializes in *explicit representations* of social class, and behaviors may include table manners and other forms of etiquette, language use, accented speech, and even physical fitness. In fact, any behavior that signals social class or is typically associated with one social class group over another would be considered a class-congruent behavior.[2]

Will's time as a graduate student provides an interesting example of class-congruent behaviors. As a graduate student, he oversaw a professional development event that prepared students for job interviews. The portion of the event that attracted the most students was the etiquette course, which focused on specific skills such as how to navigate a formal meal, how to hold a drink at a social hour, and how to conduct polite conversation. High attendance at these events signaled that many students believed they needed these behaviors and skills in order to be successful in the world of work and, perhaps, to

---

2   See also Kraus et al.'s (2017) work on class signals.

climb the social class ladder. (The Courtney Eldridge essay at the end of this chapter takes on some of these food-related behaviors.)

Anne's undergraduate years provide another example. She attended a state college in Massachusetts where she had a friend who came from a neighborhood of Boston. This friend, who majored in economics, went on to be quite successful in the world of investment management, where she was surrounded by colleagues and clients who had attended more prestigious institutions and came from towns with loftier reputations. A few years into the friend's career, she began to sense that her Boston accent was holding her back, and she paid for elocution lessons to help her lose the accent. It's interesting to note, however, that regional accents such as the Boston accent sometimes come in different flavors, each with different social class meanings. In the movie *The Departed*, for example, the Sergeant Dignam character played by Mark Wahlberg calls Leonardo DiCaprio's character a "little [expletive] snake" for having grown up with two accents, which he switched in and out of: an accent from the public housing projects of South Boston vs. one from the leafier North Shore suburbs. Indeed, people who see the world primarily through this lens of class-congruent behaviors are likely to evaluate and criticize how others demonstrate or display social class through dining manners, speech, or even gait.

People who are marginalized because of race or gender are often acutely aware of how these class-congruent behaviors play out in the macro-level EC of the dominant culture (e.g., White America), as well as in more micro-level ECs (a male-dominated workplace). Living life as a marginalized person within these ECs often means becoming highly attuned to the ways that others are acting, speaking, and carrying themselves. This attunement is sometimes a simple rule of survival and may even allow the person to "pass" in a particular context. Some BIPOC and some White people from lower-SES backgrounds can seem to shift effortlessly between the etiquette of a formal dinner to the casualness of a backyard party without much conscious effort or conflict. In other words, being successful in certain ECs often means being nimble and facile in adapting quickly to the expectations and demands of the new EC, which may well be unfamiliar territory. In fact, this flexibility can be seen as a form of capital, such as the navigational capital that Yosso (2005) describes, which involves navigating contexts that were not originally designed with BIPOC or lower-SES people in mind.

The lens of lifestyle

The last lens through which people see the self, the world, other people, and relationships involves lifestyle considerations and the ways in which people spend their time, especially their leisure time. Indeed, certain ECs and social class groups assess whether people truly belong in that group according to lifestyle factors. For example, think about the act of planning a vacation. How long is that vacation? What is the destination? Where does one stay? All of these considerations are based on social class and frequently relate to expectations of particular social class groups. Driving to Mount Rushmore and sleeping in a roadside motel may be class-congruent for some groups, but for other groups, no less than a week at the Mandarin Hotel in Paris would suffice.

Different lenses in action

Let's return briefly to the metaphor of different camera lenses. People may habitually prefer a certain lens, or it may be the case that different contexts might dictate different lenses. In his work as a counseling psychologist, Will has been affiliated with university-based counseling centers. In one, he had an undergraduate client from an affluent suburb of Chicago. She came to sessions dressed exceedingly well, with shoes, handbags, sunglasses, and clothing from designers such as Louis Vuitton and Gucci. Her "presenting problem" – that is, her reason for seeking counseling – was her inability to attract and retain friends. She also reported that others "just didn't seem to get" her and that people were jealous of her. It was such a problem, in fact, that she considered changing schools.

The client's problem was apparent after some assessment: she had a tendency to relate to herself and others through her materialism lens. Even though this tendency was somewhat adaptive and functional for her in high school and in her neighborhood back home, being at the university was a change in ECs. In this new EC, her materialism lens was tiresome and boring to those with whom she wanted to interact. Part of Will's work with this client was to help her develop ways to talk about other topics. Because her materialism script was so entrenched, she needed to practice other ways to talk with peers. As with most skills being developed, the client made some errors, but over time, her interactions with others began to improve. It turned out that this small change allowed her to feel more comfortable with herself and others.

Engage with narratives and apply the theory

Read Courtney Eldridge's essay "Thanks, but No Thanks," as well as Anne's "Stink Tree," and then apply the SCWM-R to elements of those texts using the questions provided.

Box 4.1: Essay – "Thanks, but No Thanks" by Courtney Eldridge

Listen, truth is, I don't cook, As a matter of fact, I hate to cook, I really do. I mean, I love to eat, I just hate to cook. So I married a man who cooks, and he was an amazing cook—a chef, really. Then again, great chef, lousy husband. Now there's a surprise.

Anyhow, now that I'm alone again, or rather, now that I'm single again, everything my ex taught me to cook turns my stomach. Which is a shame, really: his artichokes with vinaigrette were fantastic. His Israeli salad was a piece of cake. And that other dish . . . what's it called? It's Middle Eastern, and there are numerous variations, but all you need is a can of tomatoes, an onion, a couple eggs, and bread. . . . No, I can't remember what it's called.

Just as well, I suppose, because I can't make those things, I mean, I know how to make them, I just can't bring myself to make anything that reminds me of my ex. Which takes me back to my long history with rice. Rice and sugar. Rice and soy sauce. Rice end beans. Oh, there you go—there's something: my rice and beans are edible. Good thing, too, because that's about all I can afford to eat these days. Honestly, there are days I'm still scraping change for the subway, so, fortunately or unfortunately, cooking is the least of my worries.

You know, the other day, I was eavesreading on the subway, and there was an ad in the paper that said *Get Your Gourmet On . . .* We're talking *AM New York*, okay? Of course I had to laugh, but this whole fine dining, pop-star chef, Food TV craze, it's gone too far. But what really kills me are these people who say things like, *Oh, I could never live without great food and wine.* And on one hand, I know what they're saying, and I try not to be self-righteous, I really do. But on the other hand, I just smile, thinking, I'm sorry, but . . . do you know what an *asshole* you sound like saying that? Actually, come to think of it, my ex-husband used to say that, Gee, what a coincidence, huh? *Joke.*

All I'm saying is that we came from completely different worlds, and to be perfectly honest, there was a time that had no small appeal. I was fascinated. I mean, come on—when we started dating, I was working two or three part-time jobs, trying to write, subsisting on a steady diet of Uncle Ben's, and he was a master sommelier with a degree in restaurant management who'd moved to New York to open his own restaurant. So of course we had very different views on the place and importance of food in our lives, that was a given. What I didn't know was just how much food could unite or divide two people.

My husband summed it up in a single question, which I remember him asking while we were standing in that broom-closet-size kitchen on Chambers, shortly after we'd married. And the reason I remember is because I thought it was one of the strangest questions I'd ever heard. Were you raised on *canned food?* he said. And I'm telling you, *the look*, the shudder of disgust that ran up and down his spine as he spoke the word *canned*—obviously, something was wrong, but I had no idea what. I was just like, babe, you know the can opener's the one piece of kitchen equipment that I know how to use.

Seriously, canned food, as opposed to what, not eating? Really, what a *bizarre question*, I thought, and I almost started laughing, but all I said was, Yes, why? And then he just sort of nodded, like, oh, how *interesting.* . . . We *never* ate canned food in my house, he said, taking his plate into the other room. It sounds trivial, I know, but it wasn't—not to me, at least. Not if you knew the guy and knew how much food meant to him, what it said about a person in his eyes. And basically, I just got *slagged*, whether he meant to or not. So I stood there a moment, feeling confused, then strangely embarrassed of myself, my family. . . . So of course there was nothing to do but mock him, wrinkling my nose and repeating the comment in my snottiest tone: *We* never *ate canned food in my house.* . . .

Childish, I know: I freely admit that it was completely immature of me. But then again, it did make me feel better, mocking him, much better, actually. And the fact of the matter is that we did eat canned food in my house—and lots of it, too. What, does that make me *low class?* Fine. You know what else? Just for the record, I must have been twenty before I learned that Ragu wasn't spaghetti sauce and iceberg wasn't lettuce.

Yes, I was raised on your standard Monday-through-Friday menu of Shake 'n Bake, Spanish rice, tuna casserole, goulash, and leftovers (aka Fend-for-Yourself Night)—you know, good ol' bang-for-your-buck cooking. Out of a can, yes. I mean, seriously, *what did he think?* I told him we were poor—my family, my mother's family—I'm sorry, but isn't it common knowledge that poor means *canned*, and canned means *food* in a poor family? And you're damn glad to have it, too: that's right. Now shut up and eat.

That was my mother's family, at least, which was your basic small-town Catholic lower-middle-class family of ten. In other words, there was no discussion about *food*, are you kidding? You ate what was put in front of you; you ate everything on your plate; and you never, ever complained. Because any child who complained or refused to eat everything on their plate got their ass beat and sent to bed, hungry. That's Catholicism in my book: it's not the number of mouths to feed, it's the one who's howling, getting their ass paddled at the kitchen table. And everyone else just keeps eating, absolutely.

But of course I would say that: one of the only times in my life I was ever spanked was at the dinner table. I was about three, I guess, and one weekend, my mom made this huge pot of chili—another house specialty, chili and Fritos. And because we were broke, she made enough chili to last a week, and it did. So, by Friday night, five nights later, I'd had enough of chili, and I refused to eat my dinner. Even worse, I sassed off right to her face. *I hate chili!* I said, going so far as to shove the bowl across the table. I mean, it was just your basic bratty kid behavior, right? So I was ordered to sit there until I finished my dinner, which of course I refused to do.

So I sat at the table. And I sat. And I sat. And from time to time, my mom checked on my progress, but of course there was none. Because I had decided I would rather spend the rest of my life at that table than eat another bite of chili. It was a Mexican standoff, all right, a Knee-high Noon, and I knew I was pressing my luck. Oh, hell yeah. I knew, but I didn't care. I wasn't eating that shit.

Finally, a few hours later—and granted, it might have been forty minutes, who knows?—but at some point, my mother asked one last time if I was going to eat my dinner. *Never*, I thought, throwing myself across the table and hiding my face in my forearms, nodding, but she wasn't impressed with my performance. Keep in mind that I'd never been spanked before—my mother didn't need to raise a hand, considering she had this terrifying register of voice that said *Don't . . . fuck with me!* And that was the voice she used. This is your *last warning*. Are you going to eat your dinner? she said, firmly taking hold of my biceps. Double down, right? And I wasn't scared—it was thrilling, actually. *Last warning:* I'd never made it that far! It was the moment of truth, and I said no. *No*, I said, and that was it: snap!

I mean, *she lost it*. Oh, man, she pulled me from the table with such force that I knocked over the chair as she started wailing, paddling my ass. Honestly, if she'd had a wooden spoon, she would've broken it on the first swing. But what I remember most was her hand coming down, that there was just this haywire rhythm to her arm, like she couldn't hit me fast or hard enough, and I remember thinking—no, I somehow remember *knowing* that she couldn't stop hitting me even if she wanted to. When she finally did, I was sent to my room, and we never spoke of it again.

In all fairness, maybe she only spanked me a few times, who knows, but that is definitely how I remember it. So it was a good twenty years before we ever talked about the incident. I'm not even sure how it came up in conversation, I was probably telling her what a terrible, abusive mother she had been all my life. Oh, that's right—I cited the chili beating as but one example, and we started laughing, and then my mom finally told me the rest of the story.

The simple fact was we had no money—I mean, *no money*—no food, nothing. We had absolutely nothing else to eat in the house—no juice, no milk, bread, cereal— and my mom didn't know how she would feed me the next morning, or the next day, or the next. I don't know how she got us through that weekend; I could never ask. So yeah, she lost it. And I'm sure I would have done the same in her position. Which might have something to do with never having wanted to be in her position, but anyhow.

Now my mother is an amazing woman, truly, but she's nothing if not proud. Seriously, it took years of pleading before she allowed me to trick or treat, because she always called it the Beggars' Banquet, and *we did not take handouts.* Good Lord. Anyhow, a few years later, sometime during the late seventies, I can only imagine how difficult it was for her to apply for welfare. Then again, she had a kid, and you do what you have to do.

So we did our shopping at stores that took food stamps, and I was enrolled in one of those programs you see advertised on the subway, usually in Spanish. You know those posters with a picture of a smiling young woman and her baby or maybe just some cute little kid—*such bullshit,* but anyhow. You know what I'm talking about, those posters advertising food programs in which the low income can enroll their kids, so you can be sure your kid gets fed one solid meal a day. Which is usually breakfast, every day before school. At least that was the program I was enrolled in, and it used to shame the hell out of me, slipping out of the cafeteria every morning.

Of course it's ridiculous now, but I used to live in mortal fear that one of my classmates would see me and then the whole school, K through nine, would know that Courtney Eldridge was a welfare case . . . *oh, no!* Yes, I laugh. Then again, looking at it now, it's hard to say who was more proud, my mom or me.

I will say that my mother never encouraged or discouraged me from the kitchen. For better or worse, my guess is she never wanted me to feel the kitchen was my place—not unless I wanted it to be, and I didn't. There were just too many other things I wanted to do. But what I realized early on was that the kitchen was always the easiest place to talk to my mom, if I caught her while she was cooking, and how meditative it seemed, watching her hands chopping and stirring. I used to sit on the far counter, watching her cook, and we'd talk in a way that we never spoke anywhere else. Intimately, I suppose, for lack of a better word.

In fact, the first and only time I ever asked my mother if she believed in God was in the kitchen. I mean, I must have been twenty years old, I'd never been confirmed, my mom hadn't been to Mass in a good twenty years, and I was *still* afraid to ask. It's just one of those things we don't talk about. God and food, yes.

Now my husband, on the other hand . . . My husband was Israeli first and Jewish second, as they say. Secular, in other words. But if you ask me, all that really means is the guy had no problem complaining and no tact when doing so. Needless to say, he was extremely, I daresay violently, opinionated on the subject of fine dining in New York City. Case in point: I had to edit the word *battlefield* out of his business plan, okay? And furthermore, not only was our fine dining completely substandard, New Yorkers didn't know *anything* about great food and wine, in his opinion, and I had no choice but to hold my tongue.

I mean, there was a part of me that balked at what I considered nothing more than typical Eurotrash condescension, but then again, how could I argue? Like I said, when we met, I didn't know my Michelin from Meineke, I'm serious. Whereas my husband's entire life was spent traveling the world, staying at four and five-star hotels, dining at three- and four-star restaurants, and living a very good life, as he was always the first to point out—well, unless his mother was there to remind him first. In any case, when I said he was a chef, I didn't mean he held a culinary degree from CIA or Johnson & Wales, or any of those schools—what need? He had his mother.

Oh, I heard all about his mother, long before we met, yes. . . . Former actress, former model, semiretired world-renowned food critic—a *gastronomic writer*, to be exact. The only thing I heard about more than his mother, really, was his mother's cooking, because *no one* cooks better than my mother, he always said. And not only had she been teaching him about food and wine since infancy, the two of them had been attending special cooking schools and private classes all over the world since he was in his teens, basically.

So yes, my husband was an unapologetic snob, but not impolite. No, he was always polite in the restaurant, but I always knew what was coming, soon as we stepped out the door. This look would just cross his face, somewhere between rage and asking if the chef ate canned food growing up. But of course it wasn't just the food, it was the entire dining experience: the layout; the decor; the lighting; the service; the menu; the specials; how efficiently the kitchen was running that night; and then, the moment of truth, when the first course appeared. . . .

But his eyes would get straight to work as soon as we set foot through the front door, and he knew his business, he really did. I'll give him that any day. Sometimes, watching him take in a room, it was like watching an artist sketch a nude, the way his eyes darted back and forth, from body to canvas, never still. And sometimes he'd make a comment, offering criticism or praise, or mentioning some restaurant he knew in London or Barcelona or wherever. . . . But that's how he taught me, how I learned the most, just from watching him, really. And I was a quick study—I think so, yes.

Then again, so much has to do with exposure. He took me to all sorts of places I'd never been, restaurants I never could've afforded otherwise. Mostly two- and three-star, but the kinds of places I'd always imagined I wanted to go, until you really got down to it, and I didn't, after all. It used to cause me such anxiety, just trying to figure out what to wear, for fear of drawing attention for myself. And *why I cared*—honestly, that was such a ridiculous waste of time and energy. Really, I don't know what I was thinking. Then again, there were a few instances when my ignorance showed.

Like the first time we went to Danube, when I took my wine glass firmly in hand, pretty much like a beer bottle, I suppose, and my husband kept tapping my hand and wagging his finger at me, No no no. Until I finally said, What? What is your *problem?* I asked, completely fed up, then he leaned forward and whispered over the table, explaining that you hold a wineglass by the stem, not the bulb. I didn't know the proper way to hold my wineglass because no one had ever told me. No one had ever taught me any table manners, to be honest. So I was mortified, of course, but thankfully, there weren't too many of those incidents. And otherwise, his view of wine was this: either you like it or you don't. In fact, wine was one of the few things that humbled the guy. Which was a pleasure in itself, really.

So I decided, well, I guess I'll just tell him what I like. Soon enough, when he'd bring home a bottle of wine that really knocked my socks off, I'd call him at the restaurant, while he was working on the floor, just to tell him so. Some afternoons, he'd rush home for an hour between shifts, carrying an erect briefcase full of new wines. Oooh . . . I'd squeal, running to meet him at the door, and throwing my arms around his neck: ls that a *Blah-di-blah-y-Blah-de-blah*, or are you just happy to see me? Then, before l could lay on the full-court press of my solicitation, my husband would share the retail price, telling me not to get used to it. So, feeling slightly deflated, I'd stiffly remove my arms, telling him that if I wasn't getting used to it, he might want to look into some retail prices of his own.

Anyhow, I'd say, oh, 99 percent of the time, we agreed on wine and just about every restaurant we visited. Then again, the more I learned from my husband, the more restaurants *were* disappointing, actually. And it wasn't long before I started realizing what a snob I can be—I have it in me, I'm afraid. And then some. But the thing is, every time, every single time a word of criticism reached the tip of my tongue, I was torn between how I was raised and who I wanted to be. Which was not necessarily someone who complained in restaurants, but still.

I mean, simply admitting that my food wasn't served hot, when he asked about my entrée, felt strangely disloyal. Like I was leaving my family behind or something—it was just so against the grain . . . what can I say? It's hard to let these things go. Christ, my mother was *forty years old* before she could leave a bite of food on her plate. And I remember the day she told me, because I was so proud of her—it was a milestone in both our lives, really. Because I had to wonder how old I would be before I could do the same.

I'll tell you the turning point, though, the night everything changed for me. I mean, we went out to a lot of restaurants, and I enjoyed them, you know, but I can't say I really cared until the night my husband took me to his favorite sushi joint. Which was the night we became engaged, for all practical purposes, because this was his top-secret joint—I mean, this was a serious commitment. I'm not kidding: the guy wouldn't share the name of this place with *anyone*. But I will, of course, gladly. It's this little spot on the Upper East Side called Sushi of Gari, and I was a bit stunned when we arrived, because the place wasn't much to look at, taking our seats at the bar, while my husband ordered us the chef's special and some sake.

Of course I'd had sushi before, but this . . . Sushi of Gari was nothing less than a revelation. I know that sounds exaggerated, but I'm telling you: the man did things with fish I didn't know were possible, that were just . . . *inconceivable* to me before that moment—every single time, too. Because when you order the chef's special, you're served one piece of sushi at a time, and it's a surprise every course.

And obviously the pleasure of sitting at the bar is watching those gentleman prepare your sushi, which is genuine artistry, not to mention a complete turn-on. You know, I've often heard Anthony Bourdain bandy the word *orgasmic* about, and I'd always roll my eyes, thinking, Well, *no shit*, you're a man: that's a given. But still . . . the chef's special at Sushi of Gari is a culinary multiple orgasm. That said, I must have had twelve courses—honestly, ten, easy—before I finally said no more, thank you. And the only reason, the only reason I quit was because my husband had, and I didn't want to look like a complete pig, even though everyone behind the bar knew exactly what the score was. Even so, I could've gone all night.

Suffice it to say, looking at Gari, standing at the helm, with those dashing streaks of gray hair, looking so handsome, so stern, so, so—*masterful*, it was all I could do, biting my tongue, to keep a postcoital *I love you* from escaping my lips. I'm telling you, it was truly mind-blowing, that meal. On par with any musical, sexual and/or pharmaceutical awakening . . . ugh, I cannot imagine skydiving could be more exhilarating. Then again, the bill will certainly bring you back to earth, but anyhow. Sushi was never the same after that. Actually, nothing was the same after that.

It's true, once you know what's possible . . . Well, like they say, you can't go home again. So I figured the best way out of the jam was to take my parents, right? I mean, *I* certainly don't have that kind of money, so God bless good old Mitch and Cathy for coming to town once a year. My folks, yes, who, like me, also thought they'd had sushi before. Oh, no . . . *oh no no no,* I smiled, assuring them with my enlightened nod, if you haven't been to Gari's, you haven't had sushi, trust me, I said. And they agreed. And now, every time I speak to my dad on the phone, he always makes a point of asking about the man, if I've seen him recently, speaking in a tone as though Gari was the one I let get away.

Speaking of, rumor has it that Gari was quite taken with my mother-in-law. And who could blame him? She's stunning. She's tall, thin, she's elegant, she's led an incredibly glamorous life, and she's one of the only women I've ever known whom I'd call regal. Basically, she was everything I ever thought I wanted to be. Plus thirty years—but even that. I mean, she made aging look pretty damn good. Like somewhere you might actually want to be, one day. And at my age, she was absolutely breathtaking.

Then again, truth be told, I didn't like her at first for the simple reason that she was far more interested in talking about food than me. Hard to believe, I know, but the woman had no interest in *me*, whatsoever. It's true: we met uptown, that first night, because my husband and his mother were attending some sort of food-and-wine-pairing series at some posh midtown locale, organized by some bigwig in the French culinary scene, I don't know what. The point is, I met them for dinner at a Korean barbecue joint in the thirties. Which I strongly suspect was chosen because they allow smoking in a back room, those cunning Koreans.

So there I was, trying to make conversation with my mother-in-law asking about the tasting, which was exactly the wrong question. Because apparently, the tasting had proven a terrible disappointment, which she then proceeded to talk about on and off, the rest of the night, and I just thought, what is the big deal? So they served guacamole, and it wasn't even good guacamole. Get over it, lady. Jesus Christ. After we dropped her off at her hotel, my husband asked what I thought of her, and all I could say was, Is she *always* like that? Like what? he said. Does she always talk so much about food? Opening the building door for me, he just nodded yes, pretty much. Ohmygod, I thought, how long is she *staying?*

As it turned out, the joke was on me. Because in the end, my mother-in-law proved a far better teacher than my husband, for the simple reason that she knew how to tell a great story. She was a RADA-trained stage actress and she was so passionate about food that just listening to her was a hell of a lot more exciting and educational than any cooking show I've ever seen. Yes, she was the one who taught me that every meal tells a story, literally and figuratively, and yes, she could talk for hours about famous chefs and famous restaurants and famous meals with famous friends, many of whom are now dead, I'm afraid.

As a matter of fact, my mother-in-law was a close friend of Rex Harrison, and to this day, every time she's in New York, she makes a point of looking up Lady Marcia Harrison. They meet at Petrossian and feast on caviar, *mais bien sûr.* Oh, and by the way, it's pronounced Mar-*see*-uh, not *Marsh*-uh.

But she was no name-dropper, my mother-in-law. Really, she was no more interested in talking about a celebrity than a Parisian vendor who'd been selling her leeks since the 1960s. And of course it wasn't what, it was *how* she described the meals, how lovingly and descriptively and animatedly, all in the hopes that those people and places and meals, that those stories might live on. See, that's what I didn't get at first: that she was just trying to share something with me the best way she knew how. I guess I had so many biases of my own, it took a while for me to see that, but once I did, I finally saw the beauty in looking at the world in that light.

It certainly didn't hurt that she had some pretty outrageous stories, too. Like that one about the time Peter O'Toole visited her in Israel—that was one of the most hilarious, depraved stories she ever told. Oh, sure, he looked harmless, sitting in the back row of the Oscars a few years ago, but I'm telling you, that man is *crazy.* . . . God, she has so many stories I'd love to share, but they aren't mine to tell, you see. Regardless, my mother-in law was the first person to translate her knowledge of food into a language I could appreciate without any backlash of conscience or fear of betrayal. And I grew to love her very much.

A few months after my husband and I married, she visited and took us to a four-star restaurant to celebrate. So of course calls were made—Christ, even the whole thing with making calls and pulling favors, and I know it's partly Israeli, but even that was so strange to me—we never ask for favors in my family, but anyhow. The kitchen was notified we were coming. And it's quite a scene when one of the most famous chefs in the world steps out of the kitchen and approaches one table to speak to one guest in particular. A few minutes later, the chef leaves, of course, but people keep staring: Who are those people? Are they somebody? Should we know them? Funny.

At one point, my husband stepped outside for a cigarette, leaving me with my mother-in-law, who was telling me a story; I don't remember which, but I was rapt. So, a few minutes later, my husband returned inside, grinning, and he proceeded to tell us that one of the other guests, a senator, no less, had introduced himself outside—*Ooh hooo*, a senator, she and I said, nudging and winking at each other. We'd had a few glasses of wine by then, obviously. Anyhow, the senator laughed, offering my husband his condolences, assuming that my husband was dining with his new wife and his new mother-in-law. We all got a good laugh out of that. And it was probably the greatest compliment my husband ever paid me.

But it wasn't always like that. A year later, my mother-in-law took us to New Orleans for a long weekend. We left New York in the morning, and that cheap-ass American Airlines didn't even serve a crummy bag of pretzels, so we were *famished* by the time we got to our hotel. Well, naturally, ever the culinary explorer, my mother-in-law wanted the real deal, so we made a beeline for a famous gumbo joint near our hotel. I was so hungry by the time we sat down, I was shaking, and when our gumbo arrived, it was several bites before I realized I was the only one eating: my husband and his mother had put down their forks almost simultaneously.

When the waitress approached, asking about our food, they both smiled and thanked her, saying it was delicious. But as soon as the waitress stepped away, they began speaking in Hebrew, never a good sign. What's wrong? I asked, leaning forward. Inedible: *gruel*, my mother-in-law pronounced, with a violent shudder. I knew that shudder. Sure enough, my husband agreed, and neither touched their food, which left me in a terrible position. Waste food and go hungry, or prove myself uncouth? Tough call, yeah. Especially when, a moment later, my mother-in-law surmised, Well, it is slave food, after all. And the first thought that came to mind was *I was born a poor black child. Nothing was ever easy for me. . . .* I didn't say a word. And my stomach growled until dinnertime.

So it's probably not too surprising that I never cooked for my husband—are you kidding, between his standards and my lack of skill? Forget it. And he tried, I'll give him that—the man honestly tried to teach me to cook, at least a few of the basics, but it always resulted in a scene straight out of *The Miracle Worker*. Seriously, I can do a pretty impressive Helen Keller, when cornered, and there was my husband, trying to wrestle me down, all but throwing water on me, forcing a utensil in my hand, and signing spatula: S-P-A-T . . . What's funny is that's much too close to the truth.

Honestly, it was a running joke that eventually became a point of contention. When are you going to cook for me? he'd ask, and I'd say, Soon, soon. . . . And for a good year, two years, I had these wild fantasies of blowing him away with some dish or other, but in reality, I was way too intimidated to cook for the guy. I mean, the one thing I could make with any confidence was tuna casserole, but I knew my husband wouldn't eat tuna casserole—he'd rather starve, I'm sure of it. If he wouldn't eat gumbo, he sure as hell wouldn't eat tuna casserole.

No, I did make something for him once: I baked an apple pie, which I learned from my grandmother, who learned from her grandmother, and so of course I made it from scratch, right down to the lard. I went to the farmers' market for the apples, and Garden of Eden for the best vanilla ice cream I could find—I even made a backup piecrust, in case my first effort failed. But it didn't. No.

I'm pleased to report that my pie turned out beautifully—as a matter of fact, it was *damn good*, or so I thought, licking the knife and squeezing my shoulders, excitedly grabbing two plates. I actually surprised myself, and I was so pleased, so proud

I'd finally made something for my husband, handing him his plate, thinking, *one thing*. By God, don't ever let it be said I can't make an apple pie. . . . But I still waited, anxiously, as my husband took a bite, and he nodded that it was good, but he didn't like sweets, he said, setting the plate on his bedside table. That was it, I'm afraid.

The only other thing I, knew, that he didn't, was Mexican food. My husband had never been to Mexico; he had no idea what authentic Mexican food was about. I learned to make beans in Mexico, the second or third time I went down for any real amount of time, about ten years ago. And there's nothing to it, really, but like most things, it had never occurred to me to make them myself. But ten years later, I make some mean black beans. Now that's one thing I won't eat out of a can, beans—not even Goya brand, no way. Anyhow, by the time I had the nerve to make Mexican food, even just a couple quesadillas, I didn't care anymore. The marriage was long over.

Stillborn, really.

The one thing that makes me sad is that my mother-in-law didn't have more time to get to know my mother, and vice versa. Because these days, my mother's favorite subjects are food and cooking—and I'm so proud, I really am—because I never had a chance to see her so passionate about anything when I was growing up. By the time we finally had some money to our names—excuse me, by the time *she* finally had some money to *her* name—basically, around the time I left home, I realized my mother loved to cook.

She just turned fifty-five, and they're retiring soon, my parents. My mom's toying with the idea of going to cooking school—not in the hope of becoming a chef, but maybe catering, something like that, she says. And honestly, I don't think there's a chef in the world that could do a better job of feeding a family on nothing than she did when I was growing up. So who knows, maybe she has it in her, but I hope not. Not another chef, Mom—please, no more chefs, okay?

You know, I've been on my own for over a year now, and I still have moments when I feel torn by what I learned while I was married. For example, and I'm ashamed to admit this, sometimes I wonder if I should correct my mom and tell her how to hold her wineglass, but I never do. I mean, she wouldn't take it personally, and she might very well appreciate the tip, but it's not that easy. And *I know* it's proper, but that's just wrong in my book. I'm sorry, I will not correct my mother's manners, it's just not worth it to me.

What's interesting is that I've been reading a lot of recipes this past year—even though I only own two cookbooks, yes. The first is *How to Cook Everything*, which my parents gave me for Christmas two years ago, and which I still haven't read, actually. But the other one, the one I have been reading, is my mother's family cookbook. Aptly titled *The Eldridge Family Cookbook*, conceived by my grandfather, while we were all sitting around the dining table, during a family reunion, back in 1984. And you know what, I've hauled that little book across several continents, the past ten, fifteen years, but I'd never read the damn thing before now, no. I just needed to know it was there.

And it's just a little rectangular spiral-bound book, about eight by five and a half inches, with this white cover that my mother designed about fifteen years ago, with these little fruit and vegetable characters. . . . Never mind what it looks like—that's private. Which is why I never showed it to my husband. And as far as he's concerned, I don't regret that decision one bit, because I knew he would never understand, that he wouldn't even try. As far as I'm concerned, it's just regrettable that I didn't have the confidence to show him, to say, this is mine. This is what I come from. And please try not to wince each and every time you see mention of Campbell's mushroom soup, all right?

You know, there was a part of me that was so defiant, and a part of me that was so ashamed, and I really couldn't say which was which at any given point in time. Maybe that was fascinating to him, too, at least in the beginning. Regardless, I can see it now, how much conflict that caused, internally and externally, but I still don't understand it fully, what happened. Because the thing is, I'm not ashamed of where I come from anymore, not in the least. But I'm no longer married to the man, either. So there it is.

Sometimes, looking back at my marriage, I don't know whether to laugh or cry, really. But it was a great education, and I'll never say otherwise. And in all fairness, I'm still torn, even now. I mean, there's still a part of me that looks back and thinks, wow, I ate at Daniel. Imagine that. The girl who used to look both ways before slipping out of the cafeteria. . . . And then there's a part of me that thinks, Wow, I ate at Daniel. Big fucking deal, you know. But I remember that night, and it was a beautiful night. For once in my life I felt rich and cultured—classy, yes. I felt very, very classy. Whatever else happened between us, he gave me that, and I'm grateful, truly.

But I want a life that has plenty of room for things like Linda Logan's Party Pork Balls, or the infamous Leftover Ham Casserole. *Mmm* . . . doesn't your mouth just water? Wouldn't my ex just gag? You wonder why I've been reading recipes: there's your answer. And mark my words, one of these days, the front page of the *Times* Food Section will have a photo of some delicious-looking steamy creamy noodle concoction with the headline: *This Ain't Your Grandma Jean's Tuna Casserole*. And once again, I'll just roll my eyes, thinking, *you fuckers*. . . . There's just no winning.

Anyhow, a few weeks ago, I came across this recipe called Soda Cracker Pie, which I'd never noticed before. But it was the introduction that caught my eye: "Mother says that this really does taste like an apple pie—it was made a lot during the Depression and the recipe should be saved for posterity." Honestly, until I read that, I'd never seen the poetry, never given any real thought to how much life a recipe can hold—not ours—well, not *mine*, at least. I mean, it's been staring at me all along, and I've missed it this whole time. And that's no one's fault but my own.

So I've been thinking it's probably time I learn to cook a few things. You know, just a few things I'll willingly cook *and* eat—both, yes, that's the trick. I've even got my eye on one of the recipes in my family cookbook, my mother's salsa recipe. She's been making that salsa since I was a kid, and I'll tell you what, the woman makes some damn good salsa for a *huera*. Of course, it's also one of the easiest recipes I can find, but I have to start somewhere, right? And who knows, maybe one of these days I'll actually be able to make something Dan taught me to cook, too—but not today, no. Just not today.

Cathy's Salsa

MAKES A QUART

1 large can whole tomatoes (drain off half of the juice)
1 fresh jalapeño pepper
1 whole dried red chile or red pepper flakes
Generous shakes of cumin and powdered garlic—more generous on the cumin
1 cap of vinegar
Salt to taste

Blend all ingredients in a blender. Place in a small saucepan and bring to boil. Reduce heat and simmer for 5 minutes. Increase or decrease peppers for desired "hotness" . . . and if you have to, use canned chiles. Serve with flour tortillas.

Note: Far and away the best I've found in NYC are called, conveniently enough, Authentic Mexican brand white flour tortillas ($2.99 for eight). They put those disgusting dry white mass-market tortillas to shame. Unfortunately, the only place i know that carries them is Commodities on Second and Twelfth. And I'm happy to share my source, but there better be some tortillas there next time i make the trip. Also, I never heat tortillas in a pan with oil; I always heat them directly over the flame, flipping side every ten or fiteen seconds

Box 4.2: Essay – "Stink Tree" by Anne E. Noonan

This is usually the way it happens. I recognize the tree first by the smell, and then use my vision to confirm that I'm right. I am never wrong. This act is second nature to me, in my long-term memory, my unconscious. Wave a flowering branch under my nose while I sleep, and the tree will make its way into my dreams. Scrape my skin with something rough, and the pain message to my brain will read, for a fraction of a millisecond, "tree." Confide a loss to me, and images of my similar losses will appear; sometimes that image will be the tree.

I noticed the tree once during brunch at the house of friends, a rehabbed Victorian in Somerville, Massachusetts. I'd been walking around Nina and Bill's small fenced-in yard, mimosa in hand, and there was the aroma. It was the first time I'd come across it that June, the first time the tree's flowering season drew my attention. It took me only a few seconds to locate it, in a neighboring yard, way in the back, wedged between a high chain-link fence and a garage. I mentioned the tree later while we ate, both couples on the tiny deck, digging into another of Bill's brunches, his usual perfection served with nonchalance. What was it that day? Scrambled eggs maybe, with a slightly familiar but unidentifiable seasoning. Curried potatoes, Portuguese sausage from the grill, rugged slices of bread?

"That tree," I said, pointing. "It's such a part of my childhood in Springfield that it could be a sibling." Don looked to where I pointed, then nodded. We'd been together off and on for twelve years, married for four. He was used to my hyperbole, and he knew about my tree. Nina smiled, recognizing the shift in my tone of voice, knowing that whatever I was talking about meant something important to me.

Only Bill spoke. "You know that's the tree from *A Tree Grows in Brooklyn*, right?" He was using what I heard as his casual voice, the one for seeming ordinary, just a regular guy who happened to know some things.

"Really?" I said, trying to mask my annoyance. "I didn't know the sumac was so famous."

"Oh, that's not a sumac," he corrected.

"Yeah, I'm pretty sure it is," I said, even though I was dead certain.

"Nope," he continued. "It's an ailanthus. Tree of Heaven. The tree that grew in Brooklyn."

After a few seconds of silence, the topic changed. There was nothing left to say. Bill knew he was right, and I knew he was wrong. I knew the trees were sumacs because my mother had told me so. I never had reason to doubt her. The word itself – sumac – conveyed certainty, with its whispery beginning and definitive hard-k end. But later that day, at home with my field guide to trees, I discovered that Bill was right. The entry for sumacs sounded somewhat like my tree, but the facts about *ailanthus altissima* snapped into my memory like a Lego block.

A *rapidly growing tree with stout hairy twigs and a flat-topped crown of stout branches*, the book said.

The rapid growth sounded right. I'd go behind the neighbors' garage to rescue a ball, and there'd be several new offshoots up to my knees that hadn't been there weeks before.

Ailanthus thrives even in poor soils. Definitely. Even in the dark alleys – my shortcuts – even behind the apartment buildings and stores.

Bark is thin, dark gray, and somewhat roughened. Absolutely. I knew that roughness intimately, from slips during climbing attempts that left red, rash-like abrasions on my knees and calves.

Despite the comforting familiarity of these details, it was unsettling to learn that my mother had been wrong for all those years. I didn't know the specifics of this mistake, and I didn't call her to ask. Maybe she'd been told the tree was a sumac by her own mother, or by one of the many great-aunts we'd visit – Cora, Edith, Yvonne, Emelda, Bella. They were old, stout-chested women, most of them widowed or never married, always in stiff polyester dresses, sturdy black shoes, and thick nylons that revealed swirly patterns when the light hit them a certain way. The aunts lived in parts of the city that were less crowded than where we lived, or in surrounding towns with mills near the river, but farms and open fields further out. My mother had grown up in those places, but over time she and my father had moved closer and closer to downtown, within walking distance of his office job in the federal building.

Maybe my mother's certainty about the name was fed by her feelings about the tree, in a know-thy-enemy kind of way. She was at war with those trees. She hated having to saw down their offshoots when they threatened a fence or another tree in our backyard. She especially hated when they blossomed in June, and their tiny green-yellow flowers clumped together in puddles, and clung to windshields and trashcan lids, to the bristles of her outside broom. Most of all, she hated the smell of those flowers, and the field guide agreed: *Staminate flowers also have an unpleasant odor.*

My mother seemed to love when her work took her outdoors, to shovel snow, rake leaves, sweep the front sidewalk, or even to clean up litter blown in from the street: chip bags, candy wrappers, pages from the Morning Union. She liked trimming the lilacs, pruning her one or two rose bushes, and watering her small garden, just a few dramatic gladiolas amid unassuming petunias and marigolds; one year, a few tomato plants. But those non-sumacs and their flowers were a different story.

I, however, looked forward to the trees coming so alive in June. I loved their smell, even though I couldn't have described it if asked to. I still can't. A list of sensory words gives me only some help: earthy, yes; gamy, maybe; salty, sure; nutty, kind of. Who would understand, then or now, if I said the tree smelled like sun on skin? Or freedom? Or consolation?

The smell always meant that summer was just around the corner. My time would be unrestricted; my days of my own making. Mornings, I might do organized crafts or sports, led by city-paid college students, in the park behind our street. We made potholders with shiny metallic looms, their brightly colored paint increasingly chipped every year. We played softball and volleyball, and an improvised game called Off the Screen which used bats, baseballs, and a rusty backstop that park workers had left propped against the garage of a house abutting the park. At noon, I'd go home for lunch (maybe garden tomatoes on still-warm bread from one of the Italian bakeries), then back to the park, home again for dinner, followed by more sports outside, then peach ice cream or lemonade and chips in front of the tv after dark.

The smell of the tree meant that soon the park's enormous pool would be filled by the huge city hoses. And when the pool first opened for swimmers, the smell of the trees would be barely distinguishable from the smell of chlorine on my skin, or on my wet towel as I lay on the concrete to dry off. The smell helped me keep my crying in check that day in the driveway when my newlywed sister and her husband drove away, moving to another state. I tried to be happy for them. It was the beginning of their Beautiful New Life Together, all their silvery wedding cards said so, but it felt like an end for me. The song *When Will I See You Again* was playing on their car radio as they hugged us all goodbye. I think I was the only one to notice it.

★ ★ ★

I had wanted so badly for Bill to be wrong and my mother to be right about the name of the tree. The two of them formed a classic matchup: the Master's-from-Harvard son of Midwestern academics vs. the high-school-only daughter of French-Canadian Massachusetts millworkers. In one corner: the man for whom the tree held no real meaning other than bearing facts, things to know. In the other corner: the woman who'd used a handsaw to protect the small patches of beauty she'd created, in a neighborhood with harder edges than she would have liked. There *was* a trace of vindication in the field guide: the ailanthus is sometimes called Chinese sumac because of its origins in China and its similarity to that tree. In fact, for part of its history it had been misclassified in the sumac family. But reading further just made matters worse.

Produces many suckers; often a weed tree. Weed tree? Ouch. How could something that grows so tall (something *altissima*, the highest) be considered a weed? *Sometimes called stink tree.* Stink tree? Isn't that a little harsh? *Sometimes called ghetto palm.* Ghetto palm? Enough.

But it wasn't enough, because within a few days, I headed to the public library's fiction room to find *A Tree Grows in Brooklyn*, a book I'd never read. *You took a walk on a Sunday afternoon*, Betty Smith wrote. *You saw a small one of those trees . . . and you knew that soon that section . . . would get to be a tenement district. The tree knew. . . . That was the kind of tree it was. It liked poor people. . . . Some people called it the Tree of Heaven."*

When Francie, the book's heroine, was 11, she spent time on her fire escape with the tree's "umbrellas curled over, around and under" her, imagining that she lived in it. It was the only tree in her yard. When I was 11, I had three trees in my yard, just several feet between them, and I didn't know yet that some neighborhoods, much less mine, could be called tenement districts, or slums.

I knew that my neighborhood looked different from other neighborhoods, but I didn't think of it as deficient in any way. In fact, I thought of it as better. I felt proud having "South End" emblazoned on my softball uniform. I loved knowing that the streets immediately surrounding mine had been named the Hollywood Section decades before because single, professional people had been drawn to the brownstone apartments. We had buses, but we only needed them on rainy days because we could walk anywhere. We were closer to downtown and all the stores, and closer to the main branch of the public library, the biggest and best in the city. When I came back after summer weeks at my uncle's Cape Cod house, the neighborhood looked funny for a couple of hours, with its rows of apartment buildings and two-family houses; the discount store on one corner, and Momo's Variety on another. But it didn't look run down or depressed. It just looked different, and not un-beautiful.

I wasn't a fool. Of course I knew about differences. I knew there were people who were richer than we were, and people who were poorer. My elementary school friends and I may have been jealous of the wealthier families we knew, but we also made fun of them as uptight, out of touch, nowhere near as cool as we were. When another one of my sisters married a guy from the suburbs and then had a baby, I held court at recess with exaggerated comparisons of baby gifts from his parents and those from mine. For weeks I had them all convinced that his parents had bought the baby a huge Oldsmobile, for later when she needed it.

My school friends and I also distanced ourselves from those with less, and sometimes the person with less was one of us. Much of our teasing of one another was about money and possessions – who wore the least-fashionable clothes on no-uniform days, who had the worst house, the oldest car, the skimpiest lunches. We could be mean, no doubt, but we always knew that any insult hurled our way had a silencing retort within easy reach. You think my plaid pants on Field Day were ugly? At least you can't hear my father's muffler halfway across the city. You think my family has too many kids? At least my sandwiches have something between the slices of bread. Of course we knew about differences.

But the real discoveries came later, when high school put us in daily contact with those higher up on the ladder. Our elementary school was downtown, and it drew kids from the surrounding inner-city neighborhoods, most of whom went on to the public high schools. Those of us who stayed in the parochial system took a long bus ride to the suburban edge of the city, with its wide streets and spaced-apart one-family houses. Then we learned we were downtown kids. Then we discovered – *I discovered* – that where we lived – where *I lived* – could be called a slum. Now I had no easy comebacks if I felt disrespected or insulted.

My strategy was to try and fit in, even if it meant joking that my neighborhood was a slum, ignoring the hallway waves from kids I'd grown up with, or being vague when parents of my new friends asked, "Now exactly *where* near downtown do you live?" One day I was walking to English with Meg, a girl for whom I would have traded two or three of my downtown friends. I pointed out a hole in my sweater that I'd just noticed. She said, not unsympathetically, "Oh, too bad. That's the only nice sweater you have."

What could I have responded to that?

"I know"?

Another day, driving around the city with Melissa, a closer friend who lived in the neighborhood near high school, I suggested we go to the liquor store where nobody ever got carded. I'd become increasingly attracted to the uplift and the different-from-everyday feeling that happened when we drank beer, or from cheap bottles of wine.

"We can drink next weekend," she said, firming up her hands on the wheel.

"But why wait?" I asked. She smiled, but said nothing.

"What?" I asked.

"Nothing."

Come on, Melissa, what?" I pleaded.

Finally, after another "nothing," then more of my persistence, she gave in. "It's just that you're poor," she said, using a word I'd never heard applied to me. "And poor people can't delay gratification." After a pause she continued. "My sister learned that from one of her professors. It makes sense if you think about it."

Later, in young adulthood, there were other experiences of this feeling of lesser-ness. They targeted things I'd been taught, tacitly, to admire or respect, maybe through a barely perceptible shift in tone of voice. The university where my brother attended law school. A good job in government, a civil service job you could inhabit for life, as my father had done. Vacation weeks on Cape Cod. Back in the neighborhood, these had been signs of moving up in the world, doing well for ourselves. But gradually I found out that, far from being prestigious, these things could be, and often were, considered lesser. My brother's university was a degree mill for the working class. Government jobs were hack jobs. The Cape's nickname was the Irish Riviera.

The tree that I loved was a ghetto palm, a stink tree.

I didn't always agree with these appraisals, and I wasn't forced to take them in. I didn't have to take on the lesser-ness as mine. But some of these appraisals did color the way I saw the world. Sometimes, over evening drinks with work friends, or at brunch or dinner at their condos or houses, conversation would turn to how we'd grown up, where we'd come from. It wasn't always easy to classify, to name things correctly, to use the right words to describe growing up where and how I did.

Saying I grew up in a *slum* was complicated. Sometimes I felt triumphant owning that word, owning the swagger of it, and the punky toughness I'd developed from living in that neighborhood. After all, not everyone had a "race riot" outside of their house one summer night, really more of a street fight between guys from the longer-standing Italian families and from recently arrived Puerto Rican families. Not everyone experienced the scary thrill of hearing and seeing all those neighborhood guys that night going after each other with bats and hockey sticks. And not everyone had a neighbor shoot himself, at the end of the street closer to the projects.

However, I didn't want to mislead people into thinking that I grew up in poverty or that I was scrounging for street cred. Nor did I want to repeat what I'd done in high school: let me say slum before you do, let me laugh and call myself lesser so you don't get the chance. But romanticizing or glorifying life in the neighborhood, describing it as "true" or "honest," felt as inauthentic as quoting the Springsteen lyrics I'd sing as a teen, as I walked to or from my waitressing job. *When I strut down the street I could feel its heart beat. You're born with nothing and better off that way. Them gasoline boys downtown sure talk gritty.* And referring only to the weediness or the stinkiness of the place swept away all that was lovely: the predictability of the neighborhood, its reliable community, and the way the tree made it smell every June.

These conversations were difficult for me. I struggled with my descriptions. Sometimes I chose just to stay quiet. I was only in my twenties. I didn't know yet that sometimes things have multiple names for a reason. I didn't know that sometimes the things that are hardest to talk about become, over time, the things that scream to be explained.

Discussion questions/assignment prompts?

1 What Socialization Messages does Eldridge describe in her essay, both in childhood and in her adult life with her then-husband and his food-critic mother? What Socialization Messages does Noonan describe in her essay? Use specific textual evidence and look for explicit messages as well as implicit ones.

2 Using specific textual evidence, describe how the Social Class Worldviews of Eldridge and Noonan changed from childhood to adulthood.

3 In the essay "Stink Tree," where does the author describe shifts in her consciousness about social class and classism? Use specific textual evidence.

4 Eldrige chose not to tell her mother about the "correct" way to hold a wine glass. How do you feel about that decision? Would you decide similarly, or would you make another choice?

5 Intersectionality Check-In: In what ways can materialism and expectations to *have things* be seen as a kind of racism, a kind of sexism, or some other-ism? In what ways might materialism confine people's intersectionality, and in what ways might it help them express intersectionality?

6 Digital Spotlight: Apply any aspect of this worldview component of the SCMW-R to what you see on social media. For example, what Socialization Messages appear? How might someone's level of SCCC influence what they post? That is, would posts from someone low in awareness about social class and classism look different from

posts from someone at a higher level? Are there different forms of materialism that show up on the various platforms (e.g., clothing, homes, vacations, leisure items)?

7   What's Your Story? Choose any of the following to write about.

How has your own consciousness about social class and classism changed over the years? What specific moments in your life stand out as moments in which your Social Class Worldview shifted?

Do you have experiences as a marginalized person who needs to walk between two worlds – that is, who regularly shifts between ECs? If so, what skills have you developed in this regard and how did you develop those skills?

What is your own relationship to materialism?

References

Bronfenbrenner, U., & Morris, P.A. (2006). The bioecological model of human development. In R.M. Lerner & W. Damon (Eds.), *Handbook of child psychology: Theoretical models of human development* (pp. 793–828). Hoboken, NJ: John Wiley & Sons Inc.

Bryant-Davis, T., & Ocampo, C. (2006). A therapeutic approach to the treatment of racist-incident-based trauma. *Journal of Emotional Abuse, 6*(4), 1–22. https://doi.org/10.1300/J135v06n04_01

Dittmar, H., Bond, R., Hurst, M., & Kasser, T. (2014). The relationship between materialism and well-being: A meta-analysis. *Journal of Personality and Social Psychology, 107*(5), 879–924. http://dx.doi.org/10.1037/a0037409

French, B.H., Lewis, J.A., Mosley, D.V., Adames, H.V., Chavez-Dueños, N.Y., Chen, G.A., & Neville, H.A. (2020). Toward a psychological framework of radical healing for people of Color. *The Counseling Psychologist, 45*(1), 14–46. https://doi.org/10.1177/0011000019843506

Koltko-Rivera, M. (2004). The psychology of worldviews. *Review of General Psychology, 8*(1), 3–58. https://doi.org/10.1037/1089-2680.8.1.3

Kraus, M.W., Park, J.W., & Tan, J.J.X. (2017). Signs of social class: The experience of economic inequality in everyday life. *Perspectives in Psychological Science, 12*(3), 422–435. https://doi.org/10.1177/1745691616673192

Liu, W.M. (2011). *Social class and classism in the helping professions: Research, theory, and practice.* Thousand Oaks, CA: Sage Publications.

Liu, W.M., Liu, R.Z., Garrison, Y.K., Kim, J.Y., Chan, L., Ho, Y.C.S., & Yeung, C.W. (2019). Racist trauma, microaggressions, and becoming racially innocuous: Acculturative distress and White supremacist ideology. *American Psychologist, 74*(1), 143–155. http://dx.doi.org/10.1037/amp0000368

Mosley, D., Hargons, C.N., Meiller, C., Angyal, B., Wheeler, P., Davis, C., & Stevens-Watkins, D. (2020). Critical consciousness of anti-Black racism: A practical model to prevent and resist racial trauma. *Journal of Counseling Psychology, 68*(1), 1–16. https://doi.org/10.1037/cou0000430

Rice, A.J., Garrison, Y.L., & Liu, W.M. (2020). Spending as social and affective coping (SSAC): Measure development and initial validation. *The Counseling Psychologist, 48*(1), 78–105. https://doi.org/10.177/001100019878848

Schor, J.B. (1999). *The overspent American: Upscaling, downshifting and the new consumer.* New York, NY: Harper Perennial/Basic.

Shapiro, T., Meschede, T., & Osoro, S. (2013). *The roots of the widening racial wealth gap: Explaining the Black-White economic divide.* Waltham, MA: Brandeis/Heller School/IASP. https://heller.brandeis.edu/iere/pdfs/racial-wealth-equity/racial-wealth-gap/roots-widening-racial-wealth-gap.pdf

Sue, D.W., Alsaidi, S., Awad, M.N., Glaeser, E., Calle, C.Z., & Mendez, N. (2019). Disarming racial microaggressions: Microintervention strategies for targets, White allies, and bystanders. *American Psychologist, 74*(1), 128–142. https://doi.org/10.1037/amp0000296

Taves, A., Asprem, E., & Ihm, E. (2018). Psychology, meaning-making, and the study of worldviews. *Psychology of Religion and Spirituality, 10*(3), 207–217. https://doi.org/10.1037/rel0000201

Yosso, T. (2005.) Whose culture has capital? A critical race theory discussion of community cultural wealth. *Race Ethnicity and Education, 8*(1), 69–91. https://doi.org/10.1080/1361332052000341006

5 Classism means more than you might think

Component 3 of the SCWM-R

Accompanying Essays: Meliza Bañales, "The Poet and the Pauper"; Terri Griffith, "Winter Coat"

Check your comprehension

- A major assumption of the SCWM-R is that individuals are motivated toward social class–based Homeostasis and away from social class–based Disequilibrium.
- ECs help develop our Social Class Worldviews, and in turn, our worldviews help us understand the demands of our ECs. Capital demands and Socialization Messages play important roles.
- Individuals vary in their levels of awareness and consciousness about their social class experiences or the ways that social class operates in the world.
- Three important topics (and the ways we think about, value, and enact them) take center stage in our Social Class Worldviews: materialism and possessions, class-congruent behaviors, and lifestyle.

What do you think?

1 In Chapter 4, we discussed UMB and raised the idea that not everyone seeks to climb the socioeconomic ladder. What do you think of that idea? For the most part, do you think people want to "stay where they are" and maintain their social class position, or do you think they'd rather see themselves (or have others see them) as in a "higher" social class?

2 What about those who would rather see themselves (or have others seen them) as in a "lower" social class (e.g., the downshifters discussed in Chapter 4)? What motivates people to have that desire and to act on it?

3 Do you consider yourself a person who engages in classism on a regular basis? Why or why not?

First things first

Congratulations! You've made it to the third and final component of the SCWM-R, which focuses on different forms of classism or, as we like to say, classisms. Imagine conducting a research study exploring how people in the United States might define classism. The research goal, perhaps, would be to ask some predetermined number of people to define the term classism and maybe to describe their experiences with it. What

DOI: 10.4324/9780429317606-6

would you predict about what your respondents would tell you? Most likely, they would talk about some sort of downgrading of people deemed to be in a lower position on the socioeconomic ladder, and they may tell you about having experienced some form of classism in their lives. And those are reasonable responses, but they would only be telling part of the story.

It's helpful to recall here that the SCWM-R was developed by Will as a *theoretical* model, one created to advance thinking about how our Social Class Worldviews develop and how we internalize and experience the external structures of social class position. As a theoretical model, the SCWM-R seeks to tell a more complete story – that is, to provide a more comprehensive view of social class and classism. In that vein, the SCWM-R depicts classism as a phenomenon that involves the following: "*a behavior acted on others, an experience of discrimination to the self, and an internalized dissonance that occurs when an individual perceives him- or herself to be out of accord with others*" (Liu, 2011, p. 179). If you're thinking that this seems like a complicated definition, we hear you. This definition was created to help researchers measure classism, and the language is meant to be psychologically specific.

You may have noticed that we've used the terms classism and classisms a fair amount in this book but until now have provided the formal definition only in footnotes. Over the years of teaching undergraduate and graduate students, we've learned that backing into complicated definitions often makes the most sense, so we will do that here. We'll unpack all the pieces of the definition: the classist behaviors that are acted against others, the ways that people experience classisms being enacted against them, as well as the ways that people internalize those dynamics. And we'll also describe perhaps the most unique feature of the SCWM-R: the idea that we engage in forms of classism as a means to reinforce our perceived social class position. Our students have impressed upon us that this particular idea can be a bit difficult to grasp, so our "way into" that discussion will involve some brief review of the model.

It's all connected

As you've learned about the components of the SCWM-R, you have likely noticed some overlap between some of the components. For example, might Capital demands from one of our ECs come to us in the form of Socialization Messages? Yes, absolutely. But perhaps more important than overlap is the interconnectedness of the model's three components and the various sub-components. Thus far, we have largely discussed these components as separate, discrete units, and doing so is a helpful way to closely examine and fully understand them on their own. Now we'll do a deeper dive into some of those interconnections. Further, as we have done in previous chapters, we'll point out areas where it's especially important to consider race and racism alongside class and classisms. In the next chapter – the final chapter – Will delves even more deeply into that critical intersection of classism and racism.

As you'll recall, the first component of the SCWM-R involves ECs that range from the near-to-us micro-levels (e.g., everyday contexts such as family and neighborhood) to more distal macro-levels (e.g., overall employment rates of a country or state, or a country's capitalist economic system). ECs value certain forms of Capital (resources and characteristics) over other forms, and they expect and perhaps even demand these of us. ECs help develop our Social Class Worldviews, and our Worldviews, in turn, help us understand our ECs and interpret the Capital demands they make. ECs produce Socialization

Messages ("lessons"), and if we internalize those messages, we will likely enact them in the contexts of our ECs, which will impact others in the EC. If your family and peers are close to you, then it's likely they are in the same ECs and will funnel what they are experiencing to you as well. As we mentioned in Chapter 3, ECs can be economically homogeneous, as well as racially homogeneous, so Socialization Messages within them might be fairly homogeneous and not reflect the full array of classified or racialized experiences in the larger culture.

Now let's consider interconnections between ECs and the different "levels" of the Worldview component. It's not hard to imagine how a change of ECs (e.g., one's first professional-level job after college) might produce a shift in levels of consciousness about how social class operates. For example, the EC of the course for which this textbook was assigned will most certainly increase your awareness about social class and classism. Further, shifting to a new level of Consciousness about Social Class and Classism may well impact relations with others in your ECs. More than one student over the years has come back from Thanksgiving break joking that they nearly ruined the holiday dinner by talking about classism or capitalism.

Matters can be further complicated if our awareness about classism is increasing alongside our awareness about racism, and this is true whether we are BIPOC (Seider et al., 2019) or White people. In addition, developing more consciousness about social class might cause us to question the capital demands of an EC. For instance, learning just a bit more about how consumer debt is structured might cause someone to think twice about using a credit card to pay for a Spring Break trip just because everyone in their friend group is doing so.

Recall here that we introduced you to the SCWM-R with the tagline, "One assumption, three components." The central assumption underlying the model is that humans are motivated toward a sense of Homeostasis ("okayness") within our social class positions and motivated away from Disequilibrium with regard to social class. The model further suggests that most people shift back and forth between Homeostasis and Disequilibrium on a fairly regular basis.

Sometimes, what people are highly driven to do is to maintain their current social class positions and social status. Consider how the economic upheaval of the COVID pandemic might have complicated that task. For example, consider a family that had worked hard for years to propel themselves into a solid middle-class position and to achieve the Homeostasis that middle-class life can provide, only to find their Homeostasis threatened by the pandemic with its layoffs and business closures. Keep in mind that the term "Homeostasis" implies constancy, balance, and equilibrium, and most people prefer these states and dislike unpredictability and sudden shifts in social class–based expectations and demands.

On the other hand, sometimes what people want most is to move into another social class position and social status. For example, a middle-class family may determine that they have accrued the necessary forms of capital and economic resources to enter what they perceive to be a higher social class group – for example, the upper middle class or higher. In this case, Homeostasis can serve as an important foundation for this desired upward mobility. That is, in order to take on the new challenges of a new social class group, people have to feel secure and safe, as well as have some sense of predictability, so they may prefer to hold onto stability until they feel ready to shift out of their current situation.

For BIPOC, this notion of movement, stability, and predictability can be different from how a White middle-class family experiences it. White people moving between social class positions, especially upward, will very likely see other White people in the new EC and thus can see exemplars about how to be successful in those new social class groups. In addition to cultural similarities among White people, any barriers that may exist are more easily navigated because racism is not adding to the burden; that is, racism is not creating additional uncertainty and chaos.

Further, if we agree that racism is institutional, structural, historical, and interpersonal, then we have to see that social class groups have built-in features that explicitly and implicitly keep BIPOC from entering a new social class position or maintaining a class position. This intersection of racism and classism means that BIPOC are constantly struggling with unique demands and expectations within a new EC because of their race. They also have to cope with a loss or depletion of their resources (e.g., income) because other forms of institutional racism (e.g., at the workplace) can threaten their livelihood. In some ways too, racism can make it more difficult for BIPOC to maintain Homeostasis because the threat of Disequilibrium looms larger than it does for White people and is a more constant and real threat.

Of course, shifts into class-based Disequilibrium are not always as dramatic as the ones caused by a global pandemic. Disequilibrium can come about from a variety of sources and can happen any time someone moves into a new EC or moves into another status within the same EC. One example is a recent college graduate entering their first full-time professional job with benefits after years of part-time, unbenefited jobs in the service industry. This shift in ECs is likely to bring with it new capital demands and expectations (e.g., work apparel, workplace etiquette, professional demeanor, commitment, and loyalty to the work organization). Another example is someone being promoted into the management ranks of their workplace and experiencing new capital demands they are worried they cannot meet (e.g., Human-Capital savvy in managing the workloads of others, skill in building and maintaining Social Capital via networking).

The SCWM-R contends that being bumped into Disequilibrium will create a wish to regain a sense of Homeostasis. So, how do we go about doing that? How do we get back to that general sense of feeling okay about where we are in the social class hierarchy? More specifically, considering that this is a chapter focusing on forms of classism, what is the role of classism as we shift between Homeostasis and Disequilibrium and then back again? The short answer is that classism can cause us to feel Disequilibrium, and that probably sounds reasonable to you. But the model also contends that we *engage in* forms of classism as a means to reinforce our perceived social class position and return to Homeostasis. So, let's take a closer look at how that might work, as we discuss four specific forms of classism: Downward Classism, Upward Classism, Lateral Classism, and Internalized Classism.

Downward classism and upward classism

Downward Classism (what most people think about when they hear the term "classism") is defined in the SCWM-R as *prejudice and discrimination against those perceived to be in a lower social class position*. For example, someone might hold the attitude that people lower on the ladder are more likely to abuse drugs or act in violent ways (Colbow et al., 2016), and/or they might be reluctant to hire someone for those reasons. It's important to recognize that Downward Classism occurs across the economic spectrum. Even people who are considered among the most wealthy in society can experience Downward Classism, in addition to enacting it. For instance, in many wealthy ECs, those who are deemed to be "new money" can be seen as more materialistic, gaudy, or showy by those who consider themselves "old money," even if both groups exhibit the same lifestyle behaviors or have the same material possessions.

Similarly, Downward Classism may happen among those in the poorest situations. Sometimes people use the metaphor of "crabs in a barrel" to describe the constant downward pressure against those perceived to violate the explicit and implicit rules of a social class group, for example, trying to get ahead. For example, people may berate, tease, sabotage, and even harass a friend who tries to save money because for these peers, money needs to be spent immediately and not saved (i.e., they believe there is no benefit to saving).[1] (You may have noticed in Chapter 3 that the writer Tina Fakhrid-Deen ended her essay "Ghetto Fabulous" by using this crabs-in-a-barrel metaphor to describe the tensions of being a middle-class person in what she calls her "ghetto" neighborhood in Chicago.)

Upward Classism is defined in the model *as prejudice and discrimination against those perceived to be in a higher social class position.* Examples here might include managers at a funky nonprofit organization deciding not to hire someone who appears wealthy due to beliefs that wealthy people are selfish or out of touch (Colbow et al., 2016) or not a good fit for the organization. In the definitions of these two forms of classism, the word "perceived" is important. Let's return to the ladder tool described in Chapter 1 and revisit where you placed yourself on the ladder, especially if your placement on the ladder allows you to see the rungs below you and the rungs above you. In this way of determining that someone is higher or lower than you, Upward and Downward Classism involve a determination that others are just that – other – or are members of an "out-group" (Liu, 2011).

This "in-group" and "out-group" scenario is an important one. The different forms of classism serve to maintain the boundaries of social class groups; that is, they do the work of keeping people "in" a particular social class group and also keeping people "out." Indeed, classism is a highly relational matter in that classisms occur among people who are in relationships with one another. For the most part, we experience classisms from – and enact classisms against – those within close proximity to us rather than those more distant from us, such as the wealthiest 1% of society. And as is true with other components of the SCWM-R, the intersection of class and race dictates that for BIPOC, an experience with classism typically means an experience with racism.

Another interesting point is that – unlike the general dictionary sense of "upward" and "downward" as opposites – Downward and Upward Classism are not necessarily opposites. In two empirical investigations of this classism component of the SCWM-R, Upward and Downward Classism have been found to be related but distinct constructs, rather than opposite sides of a coin or opposite positions on a continuum (Cavalhieri & Chwalisz, 2020; Colbow et al., 2016). In other words, on any given day, we might experience Upward Classism in one EC and then Downward Classism in another. Or we might simultaneously enact Downward Classism and Upward Classism depending on context. For example, it is entirely feasible that one might agree with two of the items of the Classism Attitudinal Profile (Colbow et al., 2016) that "people who are blue collar are less refined compared to most other groups," as well as "wealthy people are out of touch with average people's experiences."

---

1 In our larger cultural conversation about poverty, people who are poor are frequently criticized for not saving their money. But when we remember that the "individual" behavior of investing is enacted within the macro-level structure of how interest rates are set up (i.e., to work more in favor of those with larger sums to invest), spending money immediately can be seen more easily as a reasonable behavior.

A further consideration with regard to Downward and Upward Classism is that, though similarly defined here, they are likely to bring about different emotional consequences for people bearing the brunt of the classism. While one may not appreciate being called "bougie" for some food choice or vacation decision, it's not hard to imagine that being called "trailer trash" is more emotionally painful. The philosopher Kwame Anthony Appiah (2018) takes this idea up in an essay about people being condescending. He offers the example of a laboratory scientist who has a minor reaction when learning that his employees find him arrogant and rude but has a more consequential reaction when someone of higher status doesn't regard him with respect. As Appiah says, "People distinguish sharply between the resentment of someone of lower status and the contempt of someone higher. One annoys; the other wounds."

Finally, it's important to recognize that the various rungs on the socioeconomic ladder are not value-neutral, especially because the rungs are merely metaphors for our actual positionality within an economic system. Simply put, people who are in a higher status – or on a higher rung on the socioeconomic ladder – have more resources and power than those on lower rungs. And the higher one goes, the easier it is to keep obtaining these resources and riches. Recall here Will's analogy of the rocket in orbit. The energy needed in orbit (higher up) to perform a task is substantially less than the energy needed on Earth (lower) to do the same task. Each rung on the ladder is not perceived as equally valuable because resources and power are so highly valued in our culture.

Examples of resources include salaries, access to higher education, better housing, safer neighborhoods, or better access to health care. Examples of power might include making donations to political campaigns in order to influence policy or social causes, or establishing organizations (e.g., The Bill and Melinda Gates Foundation) to advance a cause or a certain vision of how the world should be. Stated more simply, thus far we've used the terms "higher," "lower," and "similar," yet it's also the case that some positions in the economic system are seen as "better" (or, more dominant, privileged, or advantaged) than others because there is more access to power and resources. Conversely, some positions are seen as less desirable (or more subordinate, oppressed, or disadvantaged) because of less access to power and resources (McCormick-Huhn et al., 2019; Sensoy & DiAngelo, 2017). In Chapter 6, Will takes up these issues of power and oppression in greater detail.

Lateral classism

Consider the following example. Elizabeth lives in a suburban city in the northeast, and she and her husband are raising two young children in this locale. Their oldest is a first grader in an elementary school located in a neighborhood that was called "desirable" in the real estate listing when Elizabeth and her husband purchased their home two years ago. Elizabeth agrees that the neighborhood is lovely, but she knows most people in town would point to another neighborhood as being the most desirable. Because ECs can range from macro- to more micro-levels, Elizabeth's town can be considered an EC, as can her neighborhood and the school community. In the EC of her child's school, some families have two parents working outside of the home, and many families have just one parent working. In fact, having only one parent work outside of the home is a form of Capital considered valuable in that EC. Elizabeth and her husband both work full time. Some of Elizabeth's work days are in an office and other days she works from home. This arrangement allows her to pick up her child from school on some days.

On one of those days, Elizabeth is arranging a playdate with another mom (Sheila) who knows the school community better because she has an older child in the school. Sheila mentions another child and says of that child's mother, "You know Jen, right? She drives the black Durango." Elizabeth, in fact, doesn't know Jen, nor does she know what a Durango is. But in this brief exchange, she clearly hears two subtle Socialization Messages: (1) in this community, people are known by the cars they drive, and (2) it may be important to have a vehicle of similar worth as Jen's Durango. (You may recall from the introductory chapter that Will, in a new neighborhood, received similar Socialization Messages about lawnmowers and open garage doors.)

To be fair, not everyone might have noticed these messages. People with lower levels of Consciousness about Social Class and Classism might not have given Sheila's comments much thought. But because Elizabeth does possess a certain amount of awareness about how social class operates, she feels somewhat uncomfortable that she might be known (and worse, judged) by her automobile and its sticker price. And even though she would never call herself a materialistic person, she does briefly catch herself wondering how that sticker price stacks up against Jen's.

So how does this story fit in with classisms? You would probably answer "not really" if we asked if you see Upward Classism or Downward Classism in the Elizabeth example. Because those forms of classism involve perceptions of others being higher or lower on the socioeconomic ladder, we don't have enough evidence to make a solid call. For example, if Sheila had used the terms "bougie" or "trashy" to describe Jen's vehicle, we might have sensed Upward Classism or Downward Classism, respectively. And, indeed, these forms of classism are easier to identify than the next two forms in the SCWM-R.

While Downward Classism and Upward Classism involve looking down or up the ladder and making out-group determinations, *Lateral Classism* involves in-group determinations and looking to the side of us, that is, looking at those whom we perceive to occupy the same rung that we do. One way to think about Lateral Classism is to define it as *prejudice and discrimination against those perceived to be in a similar social class* as we are. Additionally, Lateral Classism involves *attitudes and behaviors designed to remind people of who they are in terms of social class*. Simply put, revisiting those derogatory terms "bougie" and "trashy," Lateral Classism sometimes involves trying to keep people "in their place" – that is, to call them out for acting as if they occupy a higher social class position or a lower one than they actually do.

Examples of Lateral Classism abound in the culture. For instance, you might have heard someone say that another person or a situation is "too rich for my blood." People are sometimes called bougie or are accused of forgetting "where they came from," getting "too big for their britches," or getting "above their raisin'" (Correspondents of the New York Times, 2005). Anne vividly recalls an example of Lateral Classism from the working-class neighborhood in which she grew up. There were numerous unspoken rules in that EC, for example, about how to act, or what to wear, or where families went on vacation, or what high school people should attend (one of the public schools located downtown rather than the parochial school in the suburbs). Any time someone broke one of those rules, someone from the neighborhood would ask accusingly, "What? You think you're better than us?" In all of these examples, people are being reminded to act as if they are on that same rung of the ladder as everyone else, rather than "posing" or "fronting" (or any other terms we might come up with as a culture) as a member of a different social class.

Will likes to point out that the phrase "keeping up with the Joneses" is very much about Lateral Classism, in that it urges people to spend money on the same items (e.g., vehicles) or services (e.g., lawn care) as their neighbors do. And, as is true for Downward and Upward forms of classism, Lateral Classism is highly relational in nature. In some ways, your family members, peers, and neighbors might participate in this form of classism to help you maintain your standing with them and in their perceived social class group. Further, sometimes Lateral Classism is fairly subtle and at other times can be quite extreme. In his book *For the Love of Money* (2016), Sam Polk describes the pressures he experienced as a hedge fund trader to keep making money. For Polk, the goal was to increase the number of zeros he had in his accounts and not for the actual money or what it could be used for. Polk talks about losing himself in this pursuit of money and the ways in which those around him were similarly motivated to keep making money, simply so they could compare portfolios.

Recall that in the example of the sidewalk conversation between Elizabeth and Sheila, Elizabeth sensed that a Socialization Message was being communicated to her: that in this EC of the neighborhood school, people are known by their cars and perhaps other possessions. If true, Lateral Classism may have been at work here. If Sheila perceived Elizabeth's car as of equal prestige or worth as Jen's Durango, then all was well. However, if Elizabeth's car was of lesser value, perhaps Sheila was subtly suggesting that Jen up her game in the car department. Or, if Elizabeth's car is of higher value, Sheila may have been suggesting that Elizabeth tone it down a bit. Indeed, Lateral Classism frequently polices how people "should" act in a given social class, reminding people of their inadequacies – that is, that they are being too much or not enough.

As we have asked with previous examples in this book, when we introduced Elizabeth and Sheila, whom did you see in terms of race? Were they both White? Both BIPOC? Was one BIPOC and the other White? There's no right answer to this question, of course; this is merely an example. Our point is that it's interesting and important to consider how the race of these characters would be related to how they enacted and/or experienced this example of Lateral Classism. (Perhaps you will take up this topic in one of the discussion questions at the end of the chapter.)

Internalized classism

At its heart, the SCWM-R is a theory of Worldview and how we "bring the outside in" – that is, how we internalize the social structure of social class. *Internalized Classism*, then, can be seen as the very essence of bringing the outside in. As defined in the SCWM-R, Internalized Classism involves *the feeling of frustration, dissonance, and anxiety that comes from not feeling adequate within one's own social class* (Liu, 2011). You may have noticed that, unlike the three forms of classism described earlier, the definition of Internalized Classism does not include the idea of prejudice and discrimination against others. It is a much more intra-individual phenomenon, one with several sources and several consequences, yet it is also a highly relational phenomenon that largely plays out in our relationships with others. And those other classisms are not unrelated here. As we'll demonstrate later, Internalized Classism bears a reciprocal and perpetual relationship with the other forms of classism in the model. That is, it can be brought about by experiencing classisms, and it can result in further enactments of classisms: in many ways a never-ending cycle.

Returning to the example of Elizabeth, it may be the case that Sheila's comment about Jen's car is a one-off event, just a shortcut to tell Jen apart from the rest of the parents in the community, the way one might mention her hairstyle or what street she lives on, or her role as president of the parent-teacher association. If so, Elizabeth's unease – her Disequilibrium – would likely be relatively short-lived, and she would return quite quickly to a sense of Homeostasis. However, what if Sheila's car comment is just the proverbial tip of the iceberg? What if Elizabeth encounters class-based information on a regular basis in her interactions with other parents in the EC of the school community? What if she hears frequent mentions of what kinds of cars people drive, how large their homes are, how extensive and expensive their home-renovation projects are, or how lavish families' vacation plans are? Such frequent and prolonged exposure to capital demands – these regular bumps into class-based Disequilibrium – may indeed result in Elizabeth experiencing more entrenched feelings of frustration, dissonance, anxiety, and inadequacy within her social class.

In this way, Internalized Classism can be viewed as a *consequence of prolonged Disequilibrium*. In other words, the more people are bumped out of class-based Homeostasis and into a state of Disequilibrium, the more likely they are to develop habitual, longer-standing attitudes and behaviors that become part of their sense of self. If you have enrolled in other classes that deal with structural inequality and other forms of oppression (e.g., racism, sexism), this description of classism may sound familiar. Indeed Internalized Classism bears some noteworthy similarities to other forms of internalized oppression, as will be discussed in Chapter 6.

Viewing Internalized Classism as a consequence of prolonged Disequilibrium means that anything that brings about a shift from Homeostasis to Disequilibrium might eventually result in Internalized Classism, and there are multiple possible contributors. For example, experiencing Lateral, Upward, or Downward Classisms on a regular basis might bring about Internalized Classism. Earlier we described how shifts between ECs or within ECs might result in new Capital demands and expectations that people are worried they cannot meet, and prolonged exposure to such feelings of inadequacy may result in Internalized Classism. Developing a more sophisticated SCCC may also have this impact. In fact, certain statuses within the levels of consciousness speak directly to emotions similar to those in the definition of Internalized Classism. As we pointed out in Chapter 4, the SCCC levels and statuses are not akin to a classical stage model in which gaining competence in a given level automatically confers movement to another level. In fact, it's always possible that people maintain a relatively less sophisticated Social Class Worldview, so it's important to consider how Internalized Classism might block deeper understandings about social class and classism.

Internalized Classism can also have multiple consequences. In Elizabeth's story, if the sidewalk comment about cars is just a one-off event, she may deal with her Disequilibrium in particular ways. Referring back to the idea of people having different lenses in their Social Class Worldviews, Elizabeth may engage in a number of different class-congruent behaviors in order to establish or re-establish herself as belonging in that EC. For example, she might dress in a more upscale way or hire contractors to do a major home renovation project. Alternatively, she might enact one of the classisms. She might engage in Upward Classism, for example, commenting later to her husband that Sheila seems materialistic and superficial. Or, to make herself feel better, perhaps she engages in Downward Classism, comparing her car more favorably to those driven by family members or coworkers with fewer financial resources. She may also engage in a lateral comparison of her family's overall lifestyle vis-à-vis that of other families in the neighborhood. Indeed, engaging in any of these forms of classism might return Elizabeth rather quickly to Homeostasis. But if Elizabeth is bombarded with class-based information and capital demands that she feels inadequate to address, she may be blocked from Homeostasis. It may also be the case that this prolonged exposure may cause her to develop habitual, longer-standing attitudes and behaviors that become a more entrenched part of her sense of self and her way of being in the larger world.

How did you react as you read about Elizabeth's experience of Internalized Classism? Perhaps you thought, "I'm not like that. I'm just not a materialistic person." Neither Will nor Anne consider themselves to be highly materialistic, and many of our students over the years have said this about themselves. And indeed, research studies on materialism point to substantial variation in people's self-reported levels of materialism (Dittmar et al., 2014; Gornick-Durose, 2020; Richins, 2004). Perhaps even more intriguing, there is some evidence that materialism fluctuates across the life span (Jaaspers & Pieters, 2016). Therefore, we are not arguing that everyone would experience the inner monologue or behavioral repertoire just described for Elizabeth. Nor are we arguing that people have no individual agency in the face of classism or that we are all pawns or victims in this larger socioeconomic game. There are certainly many factors that contribute to people's sense of self.

What we *are* arguing is that the pressure to purchase goods and services is a prominent feature of capitalist societies such as the United States. In fact, given that $239 billion was spent in 2019 in the United States alone on consumer advertising (Ad Age, 2020), a better question might be how can materialism *not* become part of our self-image and our Social Class Worldviews?

Engage with narratives and apply the theory

Read Meliza Bañales' essay "The Poet and the Pauper" and Terri Griffith's essay "Winter Coat"; then apply the SCWM-R to elements of those texts.

Box 5.1: Essay – "The Poet and the Pauper" by Meliza Bañales

Growing up, there were hundreds of times when I wanted to be a writer. I must have decided on it in seventh grade, when my grandparents got me an electric typewriter for my birthday. I had been writing poems on Grandma Petersen's card table and I suppose she felt there was a more productive way of doing things. That typewriter followed me until my freshman year of college, and even then it was hard to give it up to the dawning of the computer age. But I went with the times.

I have been a writer, professional and otherwise, for much of my life, and my only hope was that someday I would be good at it. I thought publishing was nice, but I knew I would be a writer whether I published or not.

In the Laundromat recently, I met a famous poet. He lives in Berkeley and writes poems about trees. He is very published, about eighty or so publications to his credit, including four books of poems. He has been interviewed for *Poets and Writers*, has taught poetry through NEA grants, and has read with some great people, like John Ashbery. I'm sure he must have felt he knew something about me when

---

he began to talk to me at the top of the wash cycle. He recognized my name, asked where I was getting my M.F.A. I told him I had just graduated from San Francisco State. He told me he remembered that I edited a magazine once, that I rejected one of his poems, but that another editor after me published one. I told him I didn't remember. I have edited magazines and scripts for a long time now, five years, and I couldn't place him right away. But I told him that I was sure his work was nice.

He asked me what I wrote. I get asked this question a lot and I never really know what to say: family, magic, poor people, brown people, mixed-race, family. It's never so black and white, I think. But people want to know, and the famous writer asked me in the Laundromat if I was published and what I was doing with my writing. I told him I had a book coming out, a book of poems. It would be out in one week. Again, he asked me what I wrote about. I told him the same subjects, and he looked at me as if he had a sour taste in his mouth. He said, "Huh, all that? There's not really a huge market for poor people. You probably won't do too well, especially since it's your first book. How did *you* get a book deal?"

The words fell, stones in a lake. They sank and the farther down they went, the more I could feel their weight, their overwhelming weight, crushing me. It was not the first time someone had told me this. I've been told by various people, in various ways, that I have nothing to say. I've been on stages all over the country and even outside of the United States and have been told to "fuck off" and asked "what do you think you're doing?" I've collected all of these and placed them as artifacts in my work, remnants of a typical life. But when the famous writer asked me the question during the spin cycle, all I could do was taste potatoes.

My mother was a master of all things potato. We grew up that broke. She would sometimes dig in trash cans for bottles and cans, because she was too proud to go on welfare. Then she would take the recycling money to the Lucky's grocery store down the street and buy a bag of potatoes. We would eat them mashed, creamed, chunky, in soup, even potato sandwiches. As a kid they stuck to my throat, never coming out.

The famous writer was still waiting for an answer. I was stuck in a bucket of memory. My brothers and I hiding our yellow tickets at school, never telling anyone we got "free lunch." Trips to Kmart to buy four children school clothes. Living in a one-bedroom apartment, one large bed supporting three tired bodies. My days spent wishing I was a real princess in a palace, eating French fries and watching cable TV in my own room. I looked for a moment, something to give the poet. But none of them seemed to make it real. I wanted to break down the racism, the classism, the outright rude nature of the poet's question, his comments like seared grease on a frying pan that just wouldn't come clean.

I wanted to let him know that I knew how to say "fuck you" without ever uttering the words. I wanted him to know what your own self-pity can taste like, how having nothing made you only want more, so much more that you were willing to imagine yourself somewhere else every day of your life. How you dreamed of being in a different-colored skin or a different culture, how you wished your father could speak more clearly, how you hated your mother for never sticking up for herself and staying in jobs that spat on her self-worth. How you saw living as a luxury and surviving as a reality. How you chewed at your own fingers until they bled and held the wounds in your mouth to remind yourself that you had control over something. The famous poet wanted me to tell him how it happened, how I came to this, to be in books and in universities; to be the judge of literature when I came from nothing, which really meant I had nothing, which equaled I was nothing.

Of course, I said nothing. I didn't tell him about the memories. Instead, I smiled. I smiled because as a woman, as a woman of color, as a poor woman of color, I didn't want to be impolite. I smiled because I wanted the poet to know that I was schooled in the art of getting by, that I had spent years learning and perfecting this smile I was giving him. The same smile my Mexican father gave to white people every time he was passed over for promotions or raises, or on the street. The same smile my mother gave her male bosses at work when they made "secretary" out to mean "personal slave," when their glances and passes at her came daily and she smiled because she had a family and no education and losing her job was just not an option. The smile my sister gave her own husband when he called her "stupid" and "fat" only hours after she gave birth to their second child. The smile my brother, Eddie, gives the cops even though he's been out of prison for years, has a good job, and is married. The smile my brother, David, gave his first-grade teacher when she told him that she would be holding him back a year because he read too slowly (she thought he wouldn't understand her speaking English to him anyway, and she didn't hesitate to tell him this to his six-year-old face). The same smile my grandparents, my cousins, my neighborhood always gave to rich white people, people of authority, whenever they were up against the wall with no chance of escape. I wanted to take all of those smiles and throw them at the poet, to let him know that I came from a different sort of education, one where you never let them know how much they get to you, never let them know how deep they've cut your soul.

But I just smiled, retrieved my wet clothes from the machine, and began placing them into another. I felt like I had failed. I hated smiling. Through all of my feminist awareness, my life experience, my existence, all I could come up with was a smile. I felt defeated and ashamed. And there were my mother's potatoes, clawing at the back of my throat, wanting desperately to come out. To throw up a potato potpie filled with the starch taste of want.

My clothes dried. I folded. I kept my mouth shut. The famous poet finished his laundry and left, waving to me as if I were an old friend. I went back to my car, where I decided that he was right: There is no market for poor people. And I returned to his question: How did *you* get a book deal?

In essence, it didn't make sense. I come from poor, working-class roots. My parents weren't college-educated. I grew up in the ghetto, the slums, the part of town people know exists but never see. I didn't write about trees, or language, or literature. For a long time, I didn't know about rhyme and meter or sound in a poem. I hadn't been brought up on the great authors of the canon and I didn't write every day because I was too busy working two jobs or trying to be the first in my family to go to college. I wrote about things I knew. I put my grandmother into my poems—her stories, her voice. I wrote about the days she spent beating her laundry against a rock and losing everything to the Dust Bowl of the 1930s. I wrote about my father's parents, who believed in magic and ghosts and the Pope and who worked in the fields of California and Texas for more than eighty years.

I wrote about my sister, her unbreakable strength, how her touch still remained tender through years of abuse. I wrote about my parents, their struggle to make every day special for us, to make it seem like we had everything we needed. How I grew up with few worries when it came to love and affection and a home that I wanted to be in. According to the famous poet in the Laundromat—the poet who had eighty publications, wrote about trees, read with John Ashbery— according to him, poetry had no room for me, for my life. According to him, nobody wanted to read about my family, my poor, brown, mestiza family. Nobody cared about roses in concrete, or love through traffic. Poetry was a place that had no room for these subjects. The fact that, amid the patriarchy, racism, classism, homophobia, and ageism of this society, I was able to get a book published that did not represent these structures, but worked against them, made me see that maybe the famous poet's question was appropriate. How did I do this. How did I get here. How did this come to be.

My answer came a few days later. That night, after doing my laundry, I went home to my boifriend, my FTM transgender boifriend (something I'm sure the poet would have asked me about as well if he had known) and cried in his arms. I told him how the poet called me out and all I did was smile. My boifriend told me it was the smartest thing I could have done. The poet wouldn't have listened to anything I said anyway. It was like that, my boifriend concluded. Smiling was not failing. In a way, I had been passing. I had been undercover. When I was discovered, smiling was all that was left because it didn't have to explain itself. It was just a smile. Take it or leave it.

Sitting down to write this, I come to an answer, and if the famous poet ever reads this he can hold me to every word. How did I get a book deal? How am I able to be in books and universities? How is it that my poems find themselves in print? I believe it's because it's poetry. Poetry is real. It encourages connections and wants attention. In the words of Muriel Rukeyser, from her book *The Life of Poetry*, "A poem invites a total response." My family, my life, is worthy of a total response. Though the oppressions of American culture remain, they are not what completely dominate a readership of poetry. I suppose I could say that my book getting published is proof that people are interested in this type of work and that there is a desire for its existence. I've spent much of my time feeling as though what I was writing was not "real" poetry. In the course of achieving three degrees, all of them in creative writing and literature, I have been told in many ways that what I write is "too ethnic," "too confessional," "too limited to only one experience," and "too raw." I was even told by a professor who I respected and looked up to as a mentor that I should reconsider going into an M.F.A. program. "Your work may not fit most programs," he told me, because it just doesn't "read like the poetry being published today." He feared I would walk away disappointed. I will say that all of these criticisms have come from white men who have numerous credentials and are taken seriously by other poets and critics. For a long time, I internalized these "critiques," this free "advice" they were giving me. These poets felt they were helping me, doing me a favor. I almost believed that they were. Reading countless anthologies, magazines, and new books of poetry, I began to see what they saw: I did not write like the poets being published today. My professor, like the famous poet in the Laundromat, was right. But I don't see this as negatively as they do. I don't want to write anything that doesn't have the power to make me think and to allow me to be the decent human being I know I can be.

I'm sure writing about trees and language and literature is very important. I'm sure there are readers out there who crave that work. But I can't write that way, I won't write that way. Why does that set me up for failure? How is writing about "real life," especially my life or how I see the world, a setup for disappointment? I want to make it clear that the longer I am kept out of the conversation of poetry, the more I don't exist. The longer my poems are encouraged to be something they're not, the more I don't exist.

I wish I could chalk up the famous poet's comments, my professor's comments, all of the comments I have received from readers who have not taken the time to truly give my work a "total response" to simple old-fashioned jealousy. I wish I had an ego that worked that way. I don't. Really. And to excuse these comments as just "poet jealousy" would be unjust. Writing off the comments as coming from a place of jealousy forces the real issues of oppression and prejudice to go undiscussed. There is a much deeper well here. If we look farther down, we will see the bottom, the place where more than water rests. I am one out of hundreds of poets who are just as talented as, if not more talented than, me, who happened to get the dumb luck of being offered a book deal at the age of twenty-five. Me: that mixed-race, Chicana, poor, working-class, queer girl who writes about her brother's lowrider and her dying grandfather. I don't know how fate decided on this. I don't know how on earth I was chosen out of all these writers to be the recipient of such luck.

But I do know that I have earned the right to the poems I imagine. I am as hard-working and broken and human as the next person, despite my complex identity. I don't claim to know everything, but I know some things and I know them well enough to explore them and honor them through poetry. I don't focus on "why me." Rather, I take it as it comes, and please know, Mr.-Famous-Poet-from-the-Laundromat, that I am worthy.

Box 5.2: Essay – "Winter Coat" by Terri Griffith

"Do you get enough to eat at home?" the school nurse asks, as she sets the clipboard in her lap and looks at me earnestly.

"Yeah," I answer, not really sure what she's getting at.

"Did your mom make you dinner last night?"

"Yeah."

"What did she make?"

"Macaroni and cheese."

"Did you have breakfast this morning?"

"Uh-huh."

"Do you have breakfast every morning?"

I don't know why the nurse is asking me these questions. I don't know why she came to my classroom and in front of my classmates asked Mr. Logan to have me excused. But it's obvious from the sound of her voice and her overly controlled tone that she thinks my mom has done something wrong. Maybe it's me who's done something wrong. Her questions make no sense. How can I give her the right answer if I can't understand why she's asking me these things? I don't want to get my mom in trouble. She wants to know what my mom feeds me. Maybe my mom cooks the wrong food. Maybe I eat the wrong things. Maybe it's because I didn't finish my vegetables last night.

"Well, I'm concerned because you're underweight. You're very small for your age."

The nurse was right about that. When I was in elementary school, I was small for my age, but it wasn't because I didn't eat. I ate fine, in a '70s sort of way. Beanie Weenie. Meatloaf with corn. Frozen fried chicken with salad. I never once went hungry. But there were a lot of times when I complained and didn't finish my dinner, especially after the third night of split-pea soup with ham hocks and carrots. Now, when I look back on the times when I think I might have gone hungry, my mom and I conveniently went to dinner at her best friend's house. For a while, we ate dinner at her house a lot.

Just four years later, in the sixth grade, I would be the second-tallest girl in the class, complete with boobs and a period. I was never the skinniest girl in my grade; Sarah was. Her parents were rich. I bet no one pulled Sarah from class to ask her what she had for dinner last night.

When I started kindergarten, not one of my classmates had parents who were divorced; I was the only one. But by the time I was in junior high, more than half the class came from single-parent homes. Without exception, all of us kids were raised by our mothers, who worked two, sometimes three jobs to support their families. It was just my mom and me, and although things seemed bad, other families had it much worse than we did.

The 1980s were hard on the Pacific Northwest economy. Many people lost their jobs, the timber industry collapsed, lumber mills closed, the salmon runs were depleted. The families in my neighborhood were all tied to these economies—families I considered rich because the kids played on soccer teams, bought their school clothes at department stores, and lived in houses their parents owned. Now I understand that these families weren't rich at all. Their fathers were longshoremen, their mothers worked at the paper mill, their family owned a fishing boat. All of these people had working-class jobs, hard jobs that extract the life from a person. I guess I was lucky when I was young—my mom had a white-collar job working for the Department of Corrections. Even though it sounds fancy, it didn't pay much—but she made ends meet. Then my mom got laid off, and life for us got much harder.

The thing about being poor is that you know what it means to be poor—and there's always someone poorer than you. For all my funky hand-me-down clothes from my mom's best friend's children, there was always some girl in class with greasy hair who smelled like pee and didn't have a winter coat.

My school didn't make it any easier to be poor, though at first glance it might have seemed as if it did. We "free lunch" kids stood in a separate line and had to give our names to the Lunch Lady, who checked us off her list. For what? To make sure we didn't get two lunches? The Lunch Lady said we had to stand in this "special" line so that she could keep track of which kids "took advantage" of their free lunch. It always felt as if we stood in that line to make sure there was no confusion between whose parents could pay for a hot lunch and whose couldn't.

The really poor kids got free breakfast too. This was the worst of all possible elementary school fates—being tagged "free breakfast." When my mom told me that I was to leave the house a half hour early so that I could have breakfast in the cafeteria, I nearly died. I didn't want to go, didn't want to face the other kids I would be joining. Their parents didn't have jobs, they came from huge families, and at least a fourth of them were from the giant government-run Children's Center, two blocks away.

These Children's Center kids had, as the principal described in a special assembly (without them), "behavioral problems," and weren't able to stay in regular foster homes with real families like other boys and girls. Back then I didn't know who those kids were. I do now. Who's labeled "incorrigible" at six? What kind of fourth-grader is unplaceable in foster care? Kids who are abused sexually and physically, kids who are drug-addicted at birth, that's who.

I was terrified of what these children might do to me. They were animals—we had been warned. Would they beat me up? Stab me in the leg with a fork? I would be one of these "free-breakfast" kids, and now everyone would know it.

At first, I simply didn't go to school early. I took my time, played in the gully, sat in the alley outside my best friend's house until she left out the back door so we could walk to school together. I waited out the breakfast portion of my day, but I was a little girl and I got hungry. Free, hot breakfast was waiting for me if I were willing to claim it.

The free breakfast my school provided was too tempting to resist. Pancakes, syrup, bacon. Scrambled eggs, sausage, cinnamon rolls. My mother's idea of a yummy breakfast consisted of bland puffed rice, dreary puffed corn, and the narcotic winter favorite, Cream of Wheat with a square of melty margarine on top. Of course, I gave in. Even so, I still had my pride. I wasn't about to give up my breakfast secret that easily. My technique was this—I shoveled the hot breakfast into my mouth as fast as possible, then shot my hand into the air and waited as the lunchroom attendant came and checked my plate to make sure I'd eaten every bite. If I ate fast enough, I could make it out of the cafeteria and into the hallway before the regular kids started arriving. That way, everyone would think I was just an early riser and not the "free breakfast" I really was.

"Cops are gone," Ricky yells from the top of the stairs.

Who knows how long we have been in that basement room, all thirty of us, crowded together, waiting in the dark, the only sound that of someone taking a slurp from their beer can. It happens all the time. The band is playing upstairs, someone spots a cop car, and we all rush to the basement before they make it to the front door. The band members always stay upstairs and pretend it is an innocent band practice that is making all the noise.

"No, officer, there isn't anyone else here. Just us." Then Ricky mumbles some promises of a quieter rehearsal, and the cops leave.

I head back upstairs to look for Kelly, a girl I can't quite call my girlfriend because we are both closeted and we only ever kiss when we both get drunk enough to make out in a back room or some car, anyplace our boyfriends won't catch us.

The two of us talk about music, smoke cigarettes, discuss what edgy book we've just read, drink even more beer, and make plans to see whatever cool band is playing in Seattle next weekend. What we never talk about is our future, what college we will go to, what we want to do for a living, what we want to be when we grow up. From where we stand, it is impossible to see our way out. We keep our talk simple. Even if we do harbor secret hopes for what our lives might someday be, we don't share them. I know it is foolish to think I can climb my way out of this ditch and into the American Dream. Eventually, Kelly will stumble back behind her drum kit and the band will start playing again (a little softer this time), until the early hours of the morning.

It's hard to plan for the future when there isn't one. What did the world have to offer us working-class kids? In the eighties, if you had money, or thought you might ever have money, you were preppy: applied to business school, liked Michael J. Fox, read books by Bret Easton Ellis. If you didn't have money and never expected to, you joined a band, went to shows on the weekend, drank cheap beer, and listened to hardcore.

With few exceptions, none of us were bad kids. Well . . . sometimes we behaved badly, but there was never malicious intent. My friends moved into "the city" (population 75,000), where I lived. They came from rural areas, towns with 5,000 people, the neighboring islands, and the reservation. A bunch of scruffy punk rockers who worked as cooks, like me, or at the lumberyard or shake mill. For some of my friends, life didn't turn out too well. Many of us ended up strung out, in prison, or dead. Some got permanent work at the paper mill or airplane factory. Others became teachers, professional musicians, and parents.

What's a young dyke with no role models to do? How could I conceptualize a future that I had never seen? I had met a couple of grown-up lesbians before. There was Butch, who worked at our neighborhood gas station. I never thought much about it, just figured she was another girl with a boy's name, like Sam or Pat or Stevie. It wasn't until high school that I realized "Butch" was probably not the name her mother gave her. Then there were the ladies who worked at the paper mill. Flannel shirts and shift work, that's what I thought being a lesbian meant. I couldn't be a lesbian; I wasn't anything like those women.

My mom raised me to be middle management, to go to college—community college first, then state college (scholarship willing). I was specifically brought up to not go to work at our town's ubiquitous factories. Pink collar over blue collar any day! I was also raised to not take risks, not because my mother thought I was incapable of taking care of myself, but because she believed that a steady paycheck was the key to a happy life, which it just might be. My mom wanted my future to contain all the things she didn't have. New clothes, the ability to pay the electric bill when it was due, the luxury of hoping to someday own my own home.

Without the protection economic stability provides, there is no room for failure. I had no room to fail. My mother had no room to fail. When a child is raised to always take the safe road, the intention is to make that child's life easier, to empower her with financial security. But really, it only teaches her that she can't do anything.

I stood on the train this morning wearing my new winter coat. I live in Chicago now, and it's the coldest place I have ever been, below-zero cold, cold that can kill you. The kind of coat you wear tells everyone on the train who you are. She's poor: She's wearing two lightweight coats that look like they came from a thrift store, or "resale shop," as they're called here. He's rich: His coat is black leather and lined with fur. She's working class: Her coat is warm and puffy, but a few years old and machine washable. In Chicago your coat is a statement of your material worth. You don't really think the stars of hip-hop videos wear those down-filled or shearling coats because they're cold, do you? Before I moved to Chicago, coats didn't mean anything to me.

Chicago has poor like I didn't even know existed—public housing projects that go on, literally, for miles; families of six living in one-bedroom apartments and people sleeping under the elevated train tracks. And there's rich like I've never seen, except on television—women and men wearing full-length furs on the street, three-hundred-dollar dinners for two, and eight-million-dollar condominiums. Oprah lives here!

My new coat cost two hundred dollars. I've never spent that much money on an article of clothing in my life—not shoes, not even a bridesmaid's dress. My coat is black wool, with shiny buttons. It's fitted, long, and has an opulent black fox collar and cuffs. I wear this coat to job interviews, out to dinner, and sometimes to parties. I will not wear this coat to bars or shows, anywhere I think will be too smoky or where someone might slop beer on it or burn me with a cigarette. This coat will be expensive to clean.

Despite its warmth and evident beauty, my coat makes me uncomfortable. I have never owned a coat so nice and I am afraid the other passengers know this too. I look around the train to see if anyone is looking at me. In this coat, I feel like a spectacle.

What do people think of me? Do they think I'm rich? Am I rich? I bought this coat, even though it was with a credit card. I'm scared to wear it too much because I don't want to wreck it, or wear it out, or spill some thing on it. My girlfriend says, "Wear the coat! It's not made of gold," though to me it is. Can the people on the train tell that I am ill at ease in something so costly? Do they think I am trying to pass for something I am not? Am I trying to pass? I worry most about what the working-class people on the train think. I want to go up to everyone wearing a faded old coat and say, "My clothes, what I have on underneath, all of it comes from the Salvation Army! Really, this is a fluke. Really, I am one of you." I don't say these things, but I think them.

Is this what growing up "without" means—that I can (almost) afford a fancy coat, but can't enjoy it? What about the American Dream, the theory that with hard work and perseverance people can transcend the class into which they are born? I want to believe in it, but I don't. Class is about more than money; it's about safety and security, knowing that what you have today, you will have tomorrow. It's about having faith and feeling safe in the knowledge that when my coat gets worn out, there will be other coats.

When I get home from work, I place my new coat on a wooden hanger, and hang it on the shower-curtain rod. I do up all the buttons, smooth it out, then go over it with a lint brush. I am going to make this coat last forever.

Discussion questions/assignment prompts

1 Bañales's essay portrays at least three of the forms of classism identified in the SCWM-R. Provide examples of each using specific textual evidence. How did each form of classism impact the author's sense of self?

2 Bañales describes classism but also describes other forms of oppression (other "isms"). Which ones? Do you think she can tease these apart, or do they seem woven together too tightly for teasing apart? Use specific textual evidence.

3 In Griffith's essay, where does she describe Internalized Classism? Provide specific textual evidence. How does this inform her sense of self?

4 At the end of her essay, Griffith shares her view of what social class is all about. What is her view? Do you see it as complete, and if not, what would you add?

5 Bañales identifies as Chicana and Griffiths is a White woman. Describe how race/ethnicity does or does not show up in these essays as both writers described classisms.

6 Revisit the essay "Stink Tree," presented with Chapter 4, in particular the "plaid pants" segment in which the author and her friends tease one another. Does that teasing to you seem to be a better example of Downward Classism or Lateral Classism? Make sure to use textual evidence to support your choice.

8 Intersectionality Check-In: Choose one or more of the forms of classism in the model and describe how that form might be experienced differently by a BIPOC vs. someone who is White. How might classisms be experienced differently by women, men, and people who identify outside of that gender binary? (Or choose another social identity/social construct more salient to you and describe how one or more of the classisms might be experienced differently.)

9 Digital Spotlight: How do you see the four Classisms show up on social media? Do you see some forms more than other forms? Why do you think that is? Are there differences between the various platforms (e.g., Instagram, TikTok)?

10 What's Your Story? Choose any of the following to write about.

How have you experienced all four of the forms of classism in the SCWM-R? If you have experienced one or two of these forms more than the others, why is that?

Can you name a time when you have used or enacted the classisms in the model? If you have used or enacted some forms more than others, why is that?

Has there been a time when you have felt you didn't live up to the social class expectations of those around you? If so, what specific emotions did you feel? Did those feelings compel you to enact any specific behaviors? Describe.

Meliza Bañales and Terri Griffith both mention their experiences with "free lunch." What was your experience with lunchtime in elementary school, and how did social class "show up" for you at lunch?

References

Ad Age. (2020, July 13). *Leading national advertisers.* https://s3-prod.adage.com/s3fs-public/2020-07/lnafp_aa_20200713_locked.pdf

Appiah, K.A. (2018, August 28). Thank you for condescending. *The New York Times.* www.nytimes.com/2018/08/28/magazine/thank-you-for-condescending.html

Cavalhieri, K.E., & Chwalisz, K. (2020). Development and initial validation of the perceived experiences of classism scale. *The Counseling Psychologist,* 48(3), 310–341. https://doi.org/10.1177/0011000019899395

Colbow, A.J., Cannella, E., Vispoel, W., Morris, C.A., Cederberg, C., Conrad, M., Rice, A.J., & Liu, W.M. (2016). Development of the classism attitudinal profile (CAP). *Journal of Counseling Psychology*, *63*(5), 571–585. http://dx.doi.org/10.1037/cou0000169

Correspondents of the New York Times. (2005). *Class matters*. New York, NY: Times Books.

Dittmar, H., Bond, R., Hurst, M., & Kasser, T. (2014). The relationship between materialism and well-being: A meta-analysis. *Journal of Personality and Social Psychology*, *107*(5), 879–924. https://doi.org/10.1037/a0037409

Gornick-Durose, M.E. (2020). Materialism and well-being revisited: The impact of personality. *Journal of Happiness Studies*, *21*, 305–326. https://doi.org/10.1007/s10902-019-00089-8

Jaaspers, E.D.T., & Pieters, R.G.M. (2016). Materialism across the lifespan: An age–period–cohort analysis. *Journal of Personality and Social Psychology*, *111*(3), 451–473. https://doi.org/10.1037/pspp0000092

Liu, W.M. (2011). *Social class and classism in the helping professions: Research, theory, and practice*. Thousand Oaks, CA: Sage Publications.

McCormick-Huhn, K., Warner, L.H., Settles, I.H., & Shields, S.A. (2019). What if psychology took intersectionality seriously? Changing how psychologists think about participants. *Psychology of Women Quarterly*, *43*(4), 445–456. https://doi.org/10.1177/0361684319866430

Polk, S. (2016). *For the love of money: A memoir of family, addiction, and a Wall Street trader's journey to redefine success*. New York, NY: Scribner.

Richins, M.L. (2004). The material values scale: Measurement properties and development of a short form. *Journal of Consumer Research*, *31*(1), 209–219.

Seider, S., Clark, S., Graves, D., Kelly, L.L., Souter, M., El-Amin, A., & Jennett, P. (2019). Black and Latinx adolescents' developing beliefs about poverty and associations with their awareness of racism. *Developmental Psychology*, *55*(3), 509–524. http://dx.doi.org/10.1037/

Sensoy, O., & DiAngelo, R. (2017). *Is everyone really equal? An introduction to key concepts in social justice education* (2nd ed.). New York, NY: Teachers College Press.

6 Social class, race, and intersectionality

A final look before we go

Anne's commentary

This final chapter looks a bit different from previous chapters. You'll notice there is no accompanying essay or comprehension check, and there are no "What Do You Think?" questions or "Discussion Questions/Assignment Prompts." Rather, we end the book with brief commentary from each of us, and then a scholarly reflection from Will about the imperative to examine social class and classism with particular attention to race and racism and other forms of oppression and intersectionality. Sometimes authors will describe their entry into a topic at the beginning of a book, but we'll do that here, briefly, at the end of the book.

Two decades ago, I conducted a study of older workers and how they experienced relationships within the workplace context. Fascinated by the power of story and the subfield of narrative psychology, I adapted a Life Story Interview to ask participants to tell their work-life stories (McAdams et al., 2001). As I listened to participants' stories for cues about the relational aspects of paid employment, I was struck by the story of one man who told his entire work history through a lens of social class. I had always been interested in the psychology of social class, and I had many internal messages churning around about my childhood experiences. (Some of those messages appear in my essay "Stink Tree," which accompanied Chapter 4.) Yet I always felt somewhat shortchanged by how my chosen discipline of psychology engaged with social class.

At the beginning of my teaching career, I discovered Will's work on the original Social Class Worldview Model (Liu et al., 2004) as well as his book describing the revised model, upon which this book is based (Liu, 2011a). Both versions of the model provided me with a framework for thinking more deeply about social class and then teaching about it at various levels of my university's undergraduate curriculum. I soon discovered that assigning creative nonfiction was a powerful way to reduce students' tendency to downplay the significance of social class, a technique that I was unable to use when facing similar blind spots in the stories of research participants. I searched in vain for a textbook that would bring together the psychology of social class and creative nonfiction narratives of social class and then approached Will to work on one together. I am grateful for this collaboration and thrilled that Will agreed to write this final chapter of the book. In it, he draws from his ongoing scholarship and further places the examination of social class and classism within larger critical contexts of race and racism, racial capitalism, Whiteness, White supremacy, and White privilege.

DOI: 10.4324/9780429317606-7

Will's commentary

I came to write, theorize, and work on scholarship around social class and classism through some serendipity. My advisor in graduate school, Dr. Donald Pope-Davis, and I talked about areas in multicultural scholarship that had not been explored. He tasked me with trying to find out what area that was. Given this challenge, I launched into an expansive and, at times, deep dive into the multicultural literature trying to understand where the scholarship lacked and where theories needed to be developed.

Over some time of reading, it seemed to me that social class and SES were areas that psychologists had not fully explored. The citations and references to social class and SES (and to a lesser extent classism) were mostly if not entirely imported from other disciplines like sociology. But aside from the intellectual challenges, social class and classism made intuitive sense to me. In other words, I had an emotional connection to it that I had not realized. Simply, I was able to understand that as an Asian American man who grew up poor, the intersectionality of gender, race, and social class were permanent aspects of my worldviews, values, and relationships. I had an intimate understanding of social class that was born from these intersectionalities that I did not see in much of the literature. I got to see aspects of this convergence when I read stories outside of psychology, and so I saw my opportunity to theorize and write about social class and classism within psychology as a chance to tell my story.

The inseparability of social class and classism

The psychological study of social class has among its many goals the development of theories that not only further research aims but also have training, education, and counseling implications (American Psychological Association, 2019; Cook et al., 2020; Diemer et al., 2013; Lott, 2002; Smith, 2005, 2009). For quite some time, this study focused on social class and classism as separate constructs that were vaguely connected to each other. With this limitation in mind, the SCWM-R (Liu, 2006, 2011a, 2011b; Liu & Ali, 2008; Liu et al., 2004) was developed as a theoretical framework that encompasses the many ways other scholars from various disciplines (e.g., sociology, anthropology, education) have discussed and described social class (e.g., consciousness, practices, upbringing; Frable, 1997; Lau et al., 2013; Liu, 2011a). The SCWM-R is different from most other theoretical conceptualizations because it explicitly connects social class with classism (Liu, 2011a). In the SCWM-R, social classes are co-created with classism, and these constructs have to be understood together because this psychological perspective (i.e., the Worldview) has to be connected to institutions that create and maintain inequality (i.e., classism). Social class, examined apart from classism, would not allow us to understand the complexities of intersectionality. Instead, social class would be construed, as it has been, as just an identity but not something constituted within a larger system of inequalities.

Social class and classism, within these institutions and systemic racism, allow us to see how worldviews and classism are implicated in interpersonal relationships. The explicit focus on classisms is important because it is not social classes, per se, that are the cause of mental and physical health problems, but rather it is experiences with classism (in all its forms) that lead to negative outcomes (Paradies et al., 2015; Rice et al., 2016). That is, one's perceived and experienced positionality and status are felt by the person as Homeostatic (an equilibrium) when there is nothing around the person to challenge and jeopardize the individual. But the psychological stresses arising from Disequilibrium can be experienced by the individual as quite disorienting and distressing, especially if they represent a constant source of pain and tension.

Moreover, because our social class position and perceived status are always unstable, the moments of Homeostasis are few. In contrast, the state of Disequilibrium can be repetitive and chronic, with long and drawn-out periods of tension that occur from perceived challenges to our position (e.g., classism). Along with these feelings of distress are the constant pursuits (e.g., social class behaviors) the person engages in to try and reclaim Homeostasis and equilibration. For some individuals, these classism experiences and the compulsions to try and resolve them are exhausting and relentless; there is always some place where interpersonal classism is being felt or practiced against another person. Classism, within a racialized capitalistic economic system, is about the perpetual need to accumulate and hoard materials, positions, experiences, and opportunities (Hagerman, 2018).

Classisms and racism

We understand classism in many similar ways that we understand racism. If we are to believe that racism is systemic and therefore a permanent feature in our society (Bell, 1993), then BIPOC are constantly experiencing forms of racism. In other words, racism exists in our environments to such a degree that an individual does not have to experience daily explicit racism, but instead, the racism experiences can come from simply knowing that racism is all around them. I describe elsewhere (Liu et al., 2019) how people internalize these ecological expectations and standards with respect to how one should be in the larger society, such that if speaking Spanish is demeaned and a source of racism, a person can carry those racist expectations around and feel marginalized without having experienced a direct racist assault. The power of racism, within a systemically racist society, is the ability to control behaviors without needing to actually act on them all the time. Similarly, classisms can be experienced or anticipated away from explicit and direct experiences with classism. The SCWM-R is similarly premised around creating psychological Homeostasis. The continued positioning of oneself within one's perceived social class and experiences of classisms (especially Internalized Classism) are the principle interpersonal mechanisms by which the individual perpetuates their perceived social class standing (Cavalhieri & Chwalisz, 2020; Cavalhieri et al., 2019; Choi & Miller, 2018; David & Derthick, 2014).

In describing all of this, what we are also proposing is that a person is constantly experiencing all forms of classism (i.e., Downward, Upward, Lateral, and Internalized), and these experiences are in a perpetual need of attention. As we mentioned earlier, there is little respite from the constant social class comparisons and, thus, the person is almost always feeling some sort of "classism." People do not live in pristine environments where they are inoculated from the intrusions of social class and classism. Rather, the individual is constantly exposed to various forms of social media, television, or news shows, and this chronic exposure to social class messages potentially triggers various forms of classism. Additionally, there is the internal psychological pressure to accumulate and hoard, which is particularly pronounced when Whiteness is factored in as well, and which I will address later. Consequently, the person is in a peripatetic state of reinstating or re-substantiating one's social class Homeostasis. This effort results in fatigue in both body and mind. The perpetual movements we embrace to relieve the social class and classism tension create a tiredness and exhaustion in our musculature. Moreover, the consistent cognitive buzzing of thinking about one's status or potential loss of status contributes to our all-ready heavy cognitive load (van Ryn et al., 2011). For many BIPOC, these forms of classism only further exacerbate the physical and psychological decline resulting from experiencing racism.

Classisms, within the SCWM-R, are critical in the creation and perpetuation of social class groups. Classisms, much like racism and sexism, are necessary co-constructs of social class, race, and gender. Social classes become real, in other words, in the individual practices and behaviors of classism (Reimers & Stabb, 2015). Specifically, classisms are the psychological and behavioral mechanisms by which we create, reify, surveil, and police the boundaries of social class groups. As described later, the perceived boundaries of social class groups are certainly racialized and gendered, and these boundaries can also represent real geographic limits as well. Neighborhood segregation, for example, allows us to see the dual operations of social class formations via classism and racism that exclude people because of their race.

Interpersonal classism and Internalized Classism (to be discussed more in-depth later) create the psychological tension and conflict that compels people to see and behave in ways that sustain social class groups and thereby maintain forms of inequality. This is not to say that there are no observable or tangible and material differences between social classes. Instead, we suggest that a person's situation, positionality, and context shape their subjective worldview about social class and how to regard observable indices like one's house or apartment, one's car, clothing, and etiquette. These observables are connected to the income, education, or occupation of a person since one does not walk around, literally, with their full income or wealth strapped to their bodies. Thus, we make interpretations, judgments, and assessments of another person's social class through our own classism lenses or Worldview. Classisms also reveal how we believe social systems operate in favor of or against a person, how we stand in relative standing to another person, and what it means to be "below" or "above" another person. We should also point out here that, for White people, Whiteness also represents a form of wealth and property (Harris, 1995) that exists outside of real income, for example. And because Whiteness can be regarded by White people as a source of wealth, their perceptions about themselves as existing atop a racial hierarchy must always be considered when interpreting experiences with classisms.

While the SCWM-R focuses on identifying and operationalizing the psychological aspects of social class and classism, it is also critical that in our conceptualizing of social class that we do not disconnect it from other identities and forms of marginalization and inequality. Social class and classism do not sit independently from other institutions of marginalization and oppression. Namely, when it comes to understanding the function of social class and classism, race and racism, and gender and sexism are integral to the formation of one's Social Class Worldview and identity, but also the experiences of classisms, racism, and sexism (Rivera & Tilcsik, 2016). Isolating social class and classism away from race and racism or gender and sexism would be intellectually and theoretically disingenuous, at best, and simply does not make sense because it will result in an undertheorization of systemic racism and oppression. Thus, when we think of terms like "systemic racism," we should automatically understand that the institutions that encourage and normalize racism are the same ones that sustain economic and racial inequality (Gómez, 2015). Social Class Worldviews and experiences with classism are not separate features of inequality, for instance, but instead, they represent the technology and mechanisms in which race and racism, as well as gender and sexism, find institutional and cultural legitimacy.

Meritocracy and legitimizing inequality

What we mean by institutional and cultural legitimacy is simply that in American society, social class and classism come with a built-in ideology that assigns effort with specific rewards. Namely, this connection of effort and rewards is mostly regarded by scholars and laypeople as meritocracy or meritocratic ideology (Liu, 2017; Liu et al., 2019). Nested within meritocracy are ideals of a "just world," as well as behaviors that are supposed to lead to success, such as the Protestant work ethic of delayed gratification and continued work. These ideologies, of course, are narratives of how to succeed in America. They give people a sense that they understand and can have control in a capitalism-driven economy. In other words, the individual level of control would be their belief in their own effort and the attendant rewards. Meritocracy and the ideology to which many of us subscribe is the dominant narrative we repeat to ourselves about how an ideal economy should function. We tell ourselves that capitalism and meritocracy would work well if racism and sexism did not abound. Instead, meritocracy really serves as the normalizing and legitimizing ideological veneer we place upon an economic system like capitalism, where this ideological obfuscation allows us to avoid the fact that capitalism is premised on racial and gender exploitation, and where systemic theft of property and wages is blamed on the individual. It is little wonder that research showing one's subscription to meritocratic values is also positively related to legitimizing inequality and non-egalitarianism (McNamee & Miller, 2009).

Our perceptions of and about social class cannot exist independently of the larger structures and systems that depend on one's subscription to these beliefs (Liu, 2011b). Thus, in conceptualizing how an individual becomes conscious and aware of social class, classisms, and economic inequality, I posit that the individual's turn away from oneself toward others also represents a cognitive shifting to understanding larger systemic forms of marginalization and oppression. But that awareness is difficult because social classes exist within a larger economic system like capitalism, where graduated expectations for how to maintain one's social class position are communicated through one's local ECs. Because we see ourselves within these smaller and more manageable communities and ECs, the expansive brutality of global capitalism seems more removed from our daily experiences. In addition, this abstraction allows for legitimizing ideologies such as meritocracy to provide a reasonable explanation for success and failures that are uncomplicated. These explanations make sense because they fit within the realm of an individual's personal experiences about themselves and their neighbors and coworkers.

Because rationalizing and legitimizing inequality comes with one's belief in meritocracy, these beliefs in meritocracy help the individual to simplistically compress and erase the intimate structural and institutional racism that created insurmountable barriers to economic success and mobility. Justifying inequality also means that those who adhere to meritocracy beliefs are unlikely to support corrective measures and policies to address centuries of racism, marginalization, and sexism. For White people in a racialized economy, the proper functioning of our systems requires BIPOC to remain in their roles within a racial hierarchy. Of course, this racial hierarchy gears the rewards of an exploitative system toward White people and thus reflects hooks's (2004) description of the United States as a "White supremacist capitalist patriarchy" (p. ix).

Racial capitalism

In describing social class and classism within capitalism, it is important that people are aware that capitalism is predicated on private ownership of resources and property, a profit–over–wage value system, and racism. Specifically, to consider oneself as a capitalist, one must also possess property and the resources on it (e.g., land) or within it (e.g., people). From a capitalist economic perspective, the means by which one acquires the property is irrelevant, and the method by which the resources are used and exploited is immaterial to the goal of profit and expanding one's ownership over additional property. Thus, one should never imbue a humanistic or moralistic framework for how capitalism operates or disregard its brutality as an anomaly. Instead, Robinson (1983) simply calls capitalism for what it is, racialized capitalism, wherein racism serves as the functioning and structuring logic for how profits are hoarded and labor and land are exploited. Because race and social class are so intimately involved, other scholars have coined new words to help substantiate this connection such as "*raceclass*" (Leonardo, 2012).

In racial capitalism, we also come to see that anti-Blackness is a worldview among those who are in power and own capital but also an institutionalized practice where laws protected and reified this form of racism (Jenkins & Leroy, 2021). Anti-Blackness is critical in understanding how social class works because without rooting our understanding in it, scholars end up seeing social class as just another identity like race rather than situating social class within systemic racism. Anti-Blackness also helps us start to see that social comparisons, and even how one perceives other people as being in a higher or lower social class, are also racialized. Similarly, for a White person, experiencing Downward Classism from another White person is a wholly different experience than experiencing Downward Classism from a Black individual.

We describe the intimate relationships of classisms and racism because so many people want to deny the interconnectedness of these two powerful constructs. In my experience, it is a fairly common occurrence that when I am talking about racism and how it structures inequality, a White audience member will bring up the importance of social class. For them, it is not race that is the most important construct, but instead, it is social class. It has also been my experience in these discussions that what the White audience member is doing rhetorically is talking about race and racism through a proxy term like social class, and furthermore, that their class analyses is, more or less, a reassertion of how meritocracy is a fair system that encourages and rewards people for their effort. Of course, what they also do not want to hear is a full excavation of meritocracy and all the psychological baggage that is tied to their belief system, and that rationalizing inequality is tantamount to legitimizing racism. Not seeing the full consequences or impact of race and racism or even just avoiding the language is, for me, the clearest definition of White privilege. Simply not contending with the weight and space that comes with always considering race and racism means that a White person is functioning normatively in White culture and in White spaces. Normativity comes with economic benefits as well as assumed positions and authority because Whiteness is already narrated into White spaces that only need embodiment.

Social class and intersectionality

As we discussed in Chapter 2, intersectionality (Crenshaw, 1989), as a method for scholarship and clinical practice, is fairly well recognized in psychology and counseling (Cole,

2009; Settles et al., 2020). With intersectionality, the focus can be on the ways in which identities may interlock to create greater forms of marginalization, oppression, and exacerbate racism. Intersectionality is not meant only to reflect multiple identities (Banks & Stephens, 2018; Liu, 2017), and we certainly recognize this imperative even while we discuss and describe social class and classisms. As we have iterated, social class and classism are inseparable from race and racism, and gender and sexism and, thus, social class and classism serve integrally to interlock identities and forms of marginalizations (Reimers & Stabb, 2015).

When we speak of social class, we are referring to the perceived and experienced groupings of people based on a subjective interpretation of economic and material criteria that forms such a grouping. Even in this definition, the interpretation of these economic and material criteria is already racialized and gendered, and anti-Blackness, for example, starts to take a prominent position. Take for instance that for some people, being considered middle-class means homeownership and that in that imagined middle class, these "homes" are structures within specific kinds of neighborhoods or what we call racialized spaces (Bonam et al., 2016; Bonam et al., 2020; Jones-Rounds et al., 2014; Liu, 2017; Liu et al., 2019). It is practically impossible to talk about homeownership or living in a particular neighborhood without recognizing the incredible historical and contemporary inequalities with respect to home loans, intergenerational wealth, redlining, property theft, and gentrification (Rothstein, 2017). All of these forms of economic marginalization are not equally distributed among BIPOC. Furthermore, while there may be similar personal experiences that White people may have with home loans, these experiences do not constitute or stem from a history of systemic and systematic exclusion and exploitation where Black families were exclusively identified to be left out of neighborhoods (Rothstein, 2017). For psychologists, this means that when we are working with individuals around their experiences with classisms, it is important to see that having a common experience does not mean that White people are experiencing *systemic* racism or exclusion.

From an intersectional perspective, classism, especially as it pertains to the unequal ways people have access to resources and materials, lays bare some robust racial differences. Taking the homeownership example, White families and Black families do not experience the same forms of classisms. Moreover, classism should not be conceptualized as only individual experiences, such as an inconvenience or poor treatment. Inconveniences and poor treatment are classism if it is linked to structural and systemic inequalities, and so in that way, a Black family's experience of being surveilled by White people as they drive through a neighborhood is vastly different from a White family's experience of being "looked down upon" because they may not look like they fit into a particular neighborhood. The Black family's experience is clearly, from an intersectionality perspective, an example of how systemic racism and classism operate efficiently together to exclude them from a valued place, but the White family has only experienced interpersonal classism.

In our discussion about intersectionality, especially as it relates to race, we clearly position Whiteness as incredibly privileged and protected as an identity. And because Whiteness is connected to multiple forms of protections and social/institutional power, White people can experience interpersonal classism but not systemic or structural classisms. Thus, because of the positionality and status afforded to Whiteness, it cannot be situated evenly or alongside Black or Latinx identities. In earlier renditions of the SCWM-R, these racial differences were not clearly articulated, and so people may have had the impression that classisms impact *all* people similarly. Here, we clarify that White people experience interpersonal classisms, but BIPOC can experience interpersonal classism that also comes with structural, institutional, and systemic forms of racism. This important distinction further makes the point that intersectionality cannot be seen simply as a matter of identity.

Internalized Classism and intersectionality

Exploring the deleterious impact of Internalized Classism through an intersectional perspective further exposes the differences that may arise because of race. Internalized Classism refers to the feelings and cognitions that arise from sensing that one is unable to maintain one's social class standing and position. Frustration, anxiety, and despondency are forms of psychological distress and tension that are triggered for people when they are finding themselves unstable within their perceived social class. Internalized Classism, within our capitalist economic structure, compels the individual to further invest in behaviors and beliefs that can help them re-stabilize their social class position. As an example, people may buy more materials they believe are relevant to those in one's perceived social class (e.g., shoes, computers, cars, clothes). Hence, Internalized Classism represents an internal compulsion to engage in deleterious behaviors and beliefs as a way to cope with the psychological tension and conflict of Disequilibrium.

In addition to experiencing Internalized Classism, only BIPOC can experience internalized racism (Cokley, 2002; Yip, 2016). The intersection of these two forms of internalized "isms" is not simply additive but is catalytic and creates not just layered experiences of oppression but something entirely synthetic and different. White people do not experience internalized racism, but they may feel and believe that they are not living up to the expectations of being a White person. Yet from a systemic racism perspective, this feeling of "letting other White people down" is just an experience of interpersonal classism since our economic structure of racialized capitalism is synonymous with White wealth, mobility, and success (Liu, 2017). Thus, there is no difference between White people feeling Internalized Classism and the feeling that they are letting other White people down. Racialized capitalism implies that racism against BIPOC was a principal feature in creating a predictable and stable economic structure for the benefit of White people (Horne, 2020). While White people are certainly exploited within capitalism (e.g., low pay and wages), they do not experience racialized capitalism or what we believe is the strain and distress that comes simply from one's race.

Intersectionality also points to the potential differences in how BIPOC respond to the catalytic outcome of Internalized Classism and racism, and how White people may respond to the psychological distress with Internalized Classism. For BIPOC, the internalized "isms" forge a psychological barrier against greater social class consciousness and racial identity awareness. Hence, we can argue that Internalized Classism and racism do not set the foundation for any sort of "liberation," but rather fortify the legitimacy of an unjust system. For BIPOC, these isms create a compelling need to further believe in the inherent morality and justice of the system in which they are embedded (i.e., system justification), as well as behaviors that BIPOC believe will allow them to restore and regain their status and positionality. In my more recent work on racial trauma (Liu et al., 2019), we posit that in some White institutional settings, BIPOC become *more* racially innocuous and racially safe around White people so they may retain their proxy privileges (i.e., contingent privileges based on their physical proximity to White people). Thus, these individuals are unlikely to voice experiences with racism or amplify their racial identification (e.g., dress differently) but are more likely to recalibrate their sensitivities in a way to better take care of White people's feelings, emotions, and cognitions around racial topics (Helms, 2016) and comfort White people who believe they are marginalized or silenced (e.g., in conversations about racial topics; Takahashi & Jefferson, 2021).

Conversely, for White people experiencing interpersonal classism, they are protected from the consequences of being racist (Helms, 2017; Liu, 2017) and thus their Whiteness allows them to potentially externalize their feelings of frustration and distress related to their inability to maintain their social class status and position. Since Whiteness and White supremacy are instrumentally linked to anti-Blackness (Horne, 2020), it is little wonder that this externalization is often directed against Black men, women, and children, as well as against other communities of Color. Being against greater immigration, social support services, and even affirmative action are ways in which White people want to preserve their racial and economic positionality. White people do see themselves as atop the racial hierarchy, and they do see themselves entitled to act to preserve that status (Mills, 1997; Mutz, 2018). For many White people, externalizing the blame for systemic racial inequalities is fairly easy to do because there are so many dominant negative stereotypes and racist narratives about how BIPOC are poor, lazy, and a financial burden on society (Jerald et al., 2017). White people who use these stereotypes are mostly protected from immediate or even long-lasting consequences for their racism (Liu, 2017). Whiteness also allows them to disregard the actual inequalities around them and to distort reality in such ways that they believe White people and BIPOC are economically similar (Kraus et al., 2019). This protection, along with White people's ability to further concretize racial inequalities as a normative function in society, is foundational to White privilege (Liu, 2017).

For White people as well, the experience of Internalized Classism means that they feel further entitled to exclude non-White others and to also hoard those materials and opportunities that will guarantee their success (Hagerman, 2018) and the success of others they perceive as White (Devos & Banaji, 2005; Kunst et al., 2018). Internalized Classism, as a White person, allows White people to rationalize exclusiveness and inequality because they see their Whiteness (and thus their status) under threat (Mutz, 2018); for White people, economic gains made by Black people are seen as a loss to them as White people and race, therefore, it is a zero-sum game (Norton & Sommers, 2011). Not surprisingly, when White people believe that resources are scarce, their perception of Black people becomes even more negative, frightening, and racist (e.g., darker skin; Krosch & Amodio, 2014; Todd et al., 2016).

This example of how Internalized Classism takes on different outcomes than just race and internalized racism shows how, in understanding the impact of social class and classism, an intersectional approach illuminates the ways that systemic racism furthers inequalities for BIPOC while protecting White people. We are able to see these different functions because classism, in the SCWM-R, is a description of how systems and institutions operate to further inequalities. In the SCWM-R, social class is the positionality and status resulting from the operations of classism (Downward, Upward, Lateral, and Iinternalized).

In summary

This chapter set out to situate the SCWM-R within the larger racialized capitalist framework by demonstrating how social class and classisms intersect with anti-Black racism, sexism, and racial capitalism to create different experiences for BIPOC and for White people. Through situating social class and classism within this larger framework, we start to see how White privilege facilitates the externalization of White people's experiences with Internalized Classism, and we also see that, for BIPOC, Internalized Classism combines with internalized racism to create more rigid and untenable positions and realities. While the SCWM-R remains an important way to theorize social class and classism, it is critically important that we examine these phenomena as they intersect with race and racism, gender and sexism, and other social identities/social constructs and positionalities. Indeed, this is how we can achieve the central work of psychologists to understand human experience in all its vastness and diversity.

In conclusion: perhaps *your story* is transformative

This textbook has relied heavily on the voices, stories, and narratives of many: psychologists, creative writers, the two of us, and – hopefully – you, through our "What Do You Think?" questions and the "Discussion Questions/Assignment Prompts." This book has also strived for an intersectional focus with regard to social class and race. In Chapter 2, we mentioned Shin and colleagues' (2017) distinction between weak (identity only) and strong approaches to intersectionality – that is, those attending to the interrelatedness of multiple social identities/social constructs while also critiquing "interlocking forms of power and privilege" (p. 460). We suggest here that our book might be categorized as having a strong approach to intersectionality. However, those authors also call for more *transformative* work, which they define as scholarship that "explicitly call[s] for the dismantling of interlocking systems of oppression" (464). We urge readers, students, instructors, and others to consider taking their interest in the psychology of social class to this next, more transformative, level. We hope that this book has elicited your narratives about your own lived experience of social class. And we further hope that some of you will use the theory and its coverage herein as a leaping off point for your own deep thinking and theorizing about one of the most meaningful cultural dimensions in people's lives.

So let us end the book with two final questions for you to consider. All along, we've been asking at the end of each chapter, What's Your Story? And now we ask this. Where might your story – your narrative of social class, classisms, and other intersecting experiences – take you? And where might that story take the field of psychology?

References

American Psychological Association. (2019). *Guidelines for psychological practice for people with low-income and economic marginalization.* www.apa.org/about/policy/guidelines-lowincome.pdf

Banks, K.H., & Stephens, J. (2018). Reframing internalized racial oppression and charting a way forward. *Social Issues and Policy Review, 12*, 91–111. https://doi.org/10.1111/sipr.12041

Bell, D. (1993). The racism is permanent thesis: Courageous revelation or unconscious denial of racial genocide. *Capital University Law Review, 22*(3), 571–588.

Bonam, C., Yantis, C., & Taylor, V.J. (2020). Invisible middle-class Black space: Asymmetrical person and space stereotyping at the race – class nexus. *Group Processes & Intergroup Relations, 23*(1), 24–47. https://doi.org/10.1177/1368430218784189

Bonam, C.M., Bergsieker, H.B., & Eberhardt, J.L. (2016). Polluting Black space. *Journal of Experimental Psychology: General, 145*(11), 1561–1582. https://doi.org/10.1037/xge0000226

Cavalhieri, K.E., & Chwalisz, K. (2020). Development and initial validation of the perceived experiences of classism scale. *The Counseling Psychologist, 48*(3), 310–341. https://doi.org/10.1177/0011000019899395

Cavalhieri, K.E., Chwalisz, K., & Greer, T.M. (2019). The role of self-efficacy in the relationship between discrimination and health care utilization among college students in the United States. *Journal of Health and Social Sciences, 4*(3), 373–388. https://dx.doi.org/10.19204/2019/thrl6

Choi, N.Y., & Miller, M.J. (2018). Social class, classism, stigma, and college students' attitudes toward counseling. *The Counseling Psychologist, 46*(6), 761–785. https://doi.org/10.1177/0011000018796789

Cokley, K.O. (2002). Testing cross's revised racial identity model: An examination of the relationship between racial identity and internalized racialism. *Journal of Counseling Psychology, 49*, 476–483. http://dx.doi.org/10.1037/0022-0167.49.4.476

Cole, E.R. (2009). Intersectionality and research in psychology. *American Psychologist, 64*(3), 170–180. https://doi.org/10.1037/a0014564

Cook, J.M., Clark, M., Wojcik, K., Nair, D., Baillargeon, T., & Kowalik, E. (2020). A 17-year systematic content analysis of social class and socioeconomic status in two counseling journals. *Counseling Outcome Research and Evaluation, 11*(2), 104–118. https://doi.org/10.1080/21501378.2019.1647409

Crenshaw, K. (1989.) Demarginalizing the intersection of race and sex: A Black feminist theory and antiracist practice. *University of Chicago Legal Forum, 1*(8), 139–167. http://chicagounbound.uchicago.edu/uclf/vol1989/iss1/8

David, E.J.R., & Derthick, A.O. (2014). What is internalized oppression, and so what? In E.J.R. David (Ed.), *Internalized oppression: The psychology of marginalized groups* (pp. 1–29). New York, NY: Springer.

Devos, T., & Banaji, M.R. (2005). American = White? *Journal of Personality and Social Psychology, 88*(3), 447–466. https://doi.org/10.1037/0022-3514.88.3.447

Diemer, M.A., Mistry, R.S., Wadsworth, M.E., Lopez, I., & Reimers, F. (2013). Best practices in conceptualizing and measuring social class in psychological research. *Analyses of Social Issues and Public Policy, 13*(1), 77–113. https://doi.org/10.1111/asap.12001

Frable, D.E. (1997). Gender, racial, ethnic, sexual, and class identities. *Annual Review of Psychology, 48*(1), 139–162. https://doi.org/10.1146/annurev.psych.48.1.139

Gómez, J.M. (2015). Microaggressions and the enduring mental health disparity: Black Americans at risk for institutional betrayal. *Journal of Black Psychology, 41*(2), 121–143. https://doi.org/10.1177/0095798413514608

Hagerman, M.A. (2018). *White kids: Growing up with privilege in a racially divided America.* New York, NY: New York University Press.

Harris, C.I. (1995). Whiteness as property. In K. Crenshaw, N. Gotanda, G. Pella, & K. Thomas (Eds.), *Critical race theory: The key writings that formed the movement* (pp. 276–291). New York, NY: The New Press/New York University Press.

Helms, J.E. (2016). An election to save white heterosexual male privilege. *Latino/a Psychology Today, 3*(2), 6–7.

Helms, J.E. (2017). The challenge of making whiteness visible: Reactions to four whiteness articles. *The Counseling Psychologist, 45*(5), 717–726. https://doi.org/10.1177/0011000017718943

hooks, b. (2004). *We real cool: Black men and masculinity.* New York, NY: Routledge.

Horne, G. (2020). *The dawning of the apocalypse: The roots of slavery, white supremacy, settler colonialism, and capitalism in the long sixteenth century.* New York, NY: Monthly Review Press.

Jenkins, D., & Leroy, J. (2021). Introduction: The old history of capitalism. In D. Jenkins & J. Leroy (Eds.), *Histories of racial capitalism* (pp. 1–26). New York, NY: Columbia University Press.

Jerald, M.C., Cole, E.R., Ward, L.M., & Avery, L.R. (2017). Controlling images: How awareness of group stereotypes affects Black women's well-being. *Journal of Counseling Psychology, 64*(5), 487–499. https://doi.org/10.1037/cou0000233

Jones-Rounds, M.L., Evans, G.W., & Braubach, M. (2014). The interactive effects of housing and neighborhood quality on psychological well-being. *Journal of Epidemiology and Community Health, 68*(2), 171–175. https://doi.org/10.1136/jech-2013-202431

Kraus, M.W., Onyeador, I.N., Daumeyer, N.M., Rucker, J.M., & Richeson, J.A. (2019). The misperception of racial economic inequality. *Perspectives on Psychological Science, 14*(6), 899–921. https://doi.org/10.1177/1745691619863049

Krosch, A.R., & Amodio, D.M. (2014). Economic scarcity alters the perception of race. *Proceedings of the National Academy of Sciences, 111*(25), 9079–9084. https://doi.org/10.1073/pnas.1404448111

Kunst, J.R., Dovidio, J.F., & Dotsch, R. (2018). White look-alikes: Mainstream culture adoption makes immigrants "look" phenotypically White. *Personality and Social Psychology Bulletin, 44*(2), 265–282. https://doi.org/10.1177/0146167217739279

Lau, M.Y., Cho, R.J., Chang, J.J., & Huang, J. (2013). Measurement and methodological issues in social class research: A call for theorization and study. In W.M. Liu (Ed.), *The Oxford handbook of social class in counseling* (1st ed., pp. 59–78). New York, NY: Oxford University Press.

Leonardo, Z. (2012). The race for class: Reflections on a critical Raceclass theory of education. *Educational Studies, 48*(5), 427–449. https://doi.org/10.1080/00131946.2012.715831

Liu, W.M. (2006). Classism is much more complex: Comment. *American Psychologist, 61*(4), 337–338. https://doi.org/10.1037/0003-066X.61.4.337

Liu, W.M. (2011a). *Social class and classism in the helping professions: Research, theory, and practice.* Thousand Oaks, CA: Sage Publications.

Liu, W.M. (2011b). Developing a social class and classism consciousness. In E.M. Altmaier & J.C. Hansen (Eds.), *The Oxford handbook of counseling psychology* (pp. 326–345). New York, NY: Oxford University Press.

Liu, W.M. (2017). White male power and privilege: The relationship between White supremacy and social class. *Journal of Counseling Psychology, 64*(4), 349–358. http://dx.doi.org/10.1037/cou0000227

Liu, W.M., & Ali, S.R. (2008). Social class and classism: Understanding the psychological impact of poverty and inequality. In S.D. Brown & R.W. Lent (Eds.), *Handbook of counseling psychology* (4th ed., pp. 159–175). New York, NY: Wiley.

Liu, W.M., Ali, S.R., Soleck, G., Hopps, J., Dunston, K., & Pickett, T., Jr. (2004). Using social class in counseling psychology research. *Journal of Counseling Psychology, 51*(1), 3–18. https://doi.org/10.1037/0022-0167.51.1.3

Liu, W.M., Liu, R.Z., Garrison, Y.K., Kim, J.Y., Chan, L., Ho, Y.C.S., & Yeung, C.W. (2019). Racist trauma, microaggressions, and becoming racially innocuous: Acculturative distress and White supremacist ideology. *American Psychologist, 74*(1), 143–155. http://dx.doi.org/10.1037/amp0000368

Lott, B. (2002). Cognitive and behavioral distancing from the poor. *American Psychologist, 57*(2), 100–110. https://doi.org/10.1037/0003-066X.57.2.100

McAdams, D.P., Reynolds, J., Lewis, M., Patten, A.H., & Bowman, P.J. (2001). When bad things turn good and good things turn bad: Sequences of redemption and contamination in life narrative and their relation to psychosocial adaptation in midlife adults and in students. *Personality and Social Psychology Bulletin, 27*, 474–485.

McNamee, S.J., & Miller, R.K. (2009). *The meritocracy myth* (2nd ed.). Washington, DC: Rowman & Littlefield.

Mills, C.W. (1997). *The racial contract.* Ithaca, NY: Cornell University Press.

Mutz, D.C. (2018). Status threat, not economic hardship, explains the 2016 presidential vote. *Proceedings of the National Academy of Sciences of the United States of America, 115*(19), e4330–e4339. https://doi.org/10.1073/pnas.1718155115

Norton, M.I., & Sommers, S.R. (2011). Whites see racism as a zero-sum game that they are now losing. *Perspectives on Psychological Science, 6*(3), 215–218. https://doi.org/10.1177/1745691611406922

Paradies, Y., Ben, J., Denson, N., Elias, A., Priest, N., Pieterse, A., et al. (2015). Racism as a determinant of health: A systematic review and meta-analysis. *PLoS One, 10*(9), e0138511. https://doi.org/10.1371/journal.pone.013851

Reimers, F.A., & Stabb, S.D. (2015). Class at the intersection of race and gender: A 15-year content analysis. *The Counseling Psychologist, 43*(6), 794–821. https://doi.org/10.1177/0011000015586267

Rice, A.J., Colbow, A.J., Gibbons, S., Cederberg, C., Sahker, E., Liu, W.M., & Wurster, K. (2016). The social class worldviews of first-generation college students. *Counselling Psychology Quarterly, 30*(4), 415–440. https://doi.org/10.1080/09515070.2016.1179170

Rivera, L.A., & Tilcsik, A. (2016). Class advantage, commitment penalty: The gendered effect of social class signals in an elite labor market. *American Sociological Review, 81*, 1097–1131. https://doi.org/10.1177/0003122416668154

Robinson, C.J. (1983). *Black Marxism: The making of the Black radical tradition.* Chapel Hill: UNC Press.

Rothstein, R. (2017). *The color of law: A forgotten history of how our government segregated America.* New York, NY: Liveright Publishing Co.

Settles, I.H., Warner, L.R., Buchanan, N.T., & Jones, M.K. (2020), Understanding psychology's resistance to intersectionality theory using a framework of epistemic exclusion and invisibility. *Journal of Social Issues, 76,* 796–813. https://doi.org/10.1111/josi.12403

Shin, R.Q., Welch, J.C., Kaya, A.E., Yeung, J.G., Obama, C., Sharma, R., Vernay, C.N., & Yee, S. (2017). The intersectionality framework and identity intersections in *Counseling Psychology* and *The Counseling Psychologist*: A content analysis. *Journal of Counseling Psychology, 64*(5), 458–474. http://dx.doi.org/10.1037/cou0000204

Smith, L. (2005). Psychotherapy, classism, and the poor: Conspicuous by their absence. *American Psychologist, 60*(7), 687. https://doi.org/10.1037/0003-066X.60.7.687

Smith, L. (2009). Enhancing training and practice in the context of poverty. *Training and Education in Professional Psychology, 3*(2), 84. https://doi.org/10.1037/a0014459

Takahashi, K., & Jefferson, H. (2021, February 4). *When the powerful feel voiceless: White identity and feelings of racial voicelessness.* https://doi.org/10.31234/osf.io/ry97q

Todd, A.R., Thiem, K.C., & Neel, R. (2016). Does seeing faces of young Black boys facilitate the identification of threatening stimuli? *Psychological Science, 27*(3), 384–393. https://doi.org/10.1177/0956797615624492

van Ryn, M., Burgess, D.J., Dovidio, J.F., Phelan, S.M., Saha, S., Malat, J., Griffin, J.M., Fu, S.S., & Perry, S. (2011). The impact of racism on clinician cognition, behavior, and clinical decision making. *Du Bois Review: Social Science Research on Race, 8*(1), 199–218. https://doi.org/10.1017/S1742058X11000191

Yip, T. (2016). To be or not to be: How ethnic/racial stereotypes influence ethnic/racial disidentification and psychological mood. *Cultural Diversity & Ethnic Minority Psychology, 22,* 38–46. http://dx.doi.org/10.1037/cdp0000046

Appendix A

Table A.1: Description of SCCC statuses as experienced by self, in relationships, and in society

1	Unawareness:	Social class is not a salient part of one's worldview. There is recognition of inequality, of rich and poor, but no real conceptualization of how social systems may work to create inequality. Overall, there may be a belief in the myth of meritocracy and an acceptance of personal and other peoples' unqualified privileges and entitlements.
	Self	The self is an independent actor in the social class system.
	Peers	Peers are perceived to reflect and endorse the individual's worldview and are believed to share a similar unaware worldview.
	Others	Some recognition that there are higher and lower "others" but no acknowledgment that the individual is also part of a larger system.
	Society	The larger socio-structural system works neutrally. People get what they deserve. The individual believes that there are some unfair advantages but not so much to unbalance the system.
2	Status Position Saliency	The individual recognizes people in higher and lower groups and the individual is aware that they belong to a social class group.
	Self	The individual generally sees themself as belonging to a social class group and begins to recognize the boundaries of their social class group.
	Peers	Peers are part of the individual's social class group and the individual recognizes peers who may belong to other social class groups.
	Others	The individual perceives multiple social class groups within which others belong, and these groups are stratified, but the individual is unclear what creates the hierarchy.
	Society	The larger society is recognized to be composed of higher and lower social class groups, some of which deserve esteem and others deserve derision.
3	Questioning	The individual questions the role of social class in their life. The questions may create anxieties and tensions related to how social class operates in the individual's life and the larger society.
	Self	Some dissonance about the individual's role in social class and inequality, generally unsure of what social class means but some burgeoning recognition that social class exists and operates. The individual may also question how they came to their particular social class position.
	Peers	Beginning sense that the individual and their cohort have certain social class boundaries, which still seem diffuse and unclear and some recognition that the peer group has boundaries.
	Others	Steady recognition that there are social class in-groups and out-groups.

	Society	Still greatly unsure how the larger socio-structural system of social class operates but some sense that status considerations are important parts of one's experience.
4	Exploration and Justification	The individual seeks out knowledge and experiences to answer these questions. The individual is primarily interested in finding support for their previously held beliefs about how social class functions and the role it plays in their life.
	Self	The self is unsure and is vulnerable, but the individual is willing to explore answers that may support their already existing, albeit tenuous, worldview.
	Peers	Peers and the cohort group are sought out for answers but a growing recognition that the peer group may be an unreliable source of information.
	Others	Other people are unreliable because they do not "understand" the individual's experiences and perspectives and are likely to challenge the individual too much.
	Society	A growing sense that society "must" be just and inequality "must" be a "natural" product of people's efforts.
5	Despair	The individual resigns themself to believing there is no escape from the current circumstances. For instance, an individual in poverty may believe they cannot move beyond their situation.
	Self	The self is perceived as impotent against the current situation; the individual does not believe they possess the skills to overcome their situation.
	Peers	Peers are regarded in a similar situation and peers may be the target of anger if they try to deviate (improve) their current situation.
	Others	People are not interested in helping you cope with the situation better.
	Society	There are rich and poor and society is made to make the rich richer and the poor poorer.
6	The World Is Just	The individual is resigned to accepting inequality and the rationalization that people get what they deserve. The individual is interested in their own privilege, entitlements, and status attainment.
	Self	Because the world is unchangeable, it is important to look out for oneself.
	Peers	Peers are sought out who reinforce this same worldview. Usually, people reinforce the individual's current social class position or who are interested in upward mobility.
	Others	Other people have not worked hard enough or made the right "life choices" to succeed.
	Society	Society is just and inequality is a natural product and process.
7	Intellectualized Anger and Frustration	As the individual explores their questions around social class, classism, and inequality, the individual becomes angry and frustrated at the state of inequality. The individual becomes increasingly interested in addressing economic inequality. The individual likely attempts to involve themself in broad and far-reaching activities that are outside their ability to intervene and understand. There is no introspection and deep consideration about poverty and inequality except reactive anger and frustration.
	Self	The self is blameless, and it is others and society who created inequality, and it is the individual who must "correct" the injustices.

	Peers	Interested in seeking out other groups and expanding their peer group to find additional support for their experiences and growing perspective. Peers are expected to reflect the individual's worldview about inequality.
	Others	Others are lumped into oppressed and oppressors
	Society	Society is unjust and must be corrected
8	Reinvestment	The individual investigates social class, classism, and inequality again in their own personal life and explores how their actions impact others. The individual is interested in finding ways to understand social class in their own world.
	Self	The individual recognizes that they are engaged in unequal, unjust, and sometimes classist actions. The individual recognizes these actions as having negative impacts on others. They begin to connect individual behavior to possibly larger social problems.
	Peers	The individual observes how peers also enact social class and classism. Peers are being evaluated on their social class consciousness.
	Others	Rather than focusing on society at large, the individual focuses on their surrounding environment. The individual's interest is the immediate context within which social class and classism are enacted and how their individual behaviors may make an impact.
	Society	Society is recognized to be composed of smaller contexts. These smaller contexts are the ways in which society may be changed to be more equitable.
9	Engagement	The individual is actively involved in social class, inequality, and poverty issues in their community. The individual is testing their developing awareness of being a socially classed person.
	Self	The individual recognizes the importance of being vigilant against inequality and that social class operates all around. The individual is intentional and deliberate about how they act in certain contexts, are sensitive to social class differences.
	Peers	New peer groups may be sought that reinforce this growing new consciousness. Dissonance and conflict may still exist as the individual shifts away from old friends to new networks. Anxiety may increase from these new experiences.
	Others	It is important to find a way to help people in one's community/ neighborhood. It is also important to support other causes against classism.
	Society	Society is largely unjust and classist and marginalizing of people who come from poverty and the poor. The whole of society cannot be changed immediately, but it is important to be a part of or start a process of change.
10	Equilibration	The individual is able to complexly explore and understand the role of social class in their world. The individual struggles for equilibrium when trying to figure out issues of poverty/injustice.
	Self	The individual recognizes that they are constantly negotiating privilege and power, and there are some times and contexts in which they have and use the privilege and others in which they do not or cannot exercise privilege.
	Peers	The individual has multiple groups of friends and peers, which reflects their complex understanding of social class. The individual has some ability to move between and within each of these groups.

Others	The individual recognizes people in different strata and sees the privileges, power, and limits of each group. They recognize the fluidity of these groups and how context changes the quality of each group.
Society	Society is not an independent entity or organism outside the individual, and the individual can only make changes through constant vigilance in combating classism.

Index